# Measures

1 tablespoon = 3 teaspoons
4 tablespoons = 1/4 cup
1 cup = 250 ml
1 pint = 500 ml
1 quart = 0.95 L
1 gallon = 3.8 L

1 teaspoon = 5 ml
1 tablespoon or 1/2 fluid ounce =15 ml
1 fluid ounce or 1/8 cup= 30 ml
1/4 cup or 2 fluid ounces =60 ml
1/3 cup= 80 ml
1/2 cup or 4 fluid ounces=120 ml
2/3 cup=160 ml
3/4 cup or 6 fluid ounces=180 ml
1 cup or 8 fluid ounces or half a pint= 240 ml
2 cups or 1 pint or 16 fluid ounces =475 ml
4 cups or 2 pints or 1 quart = 950 ml

1 ounce = 28 g
4 ounces or 1/4 pound =113 g
1/3 pound=150 g
8 ounces or 1/2 pound =230 g
2/3 pound =300 g
12 ounces or 3/4 pound =340 g
1 pound or 16 ounces =450 g
2 pounds= 900 g

# Contents

VEGETABLE COMBINATIONS

NUT DISHES

RICE, MACARONI, ETC.

CROQUETTES

TIMBALES AND PATTIES

SAUCES

EGG DISHES

CHEESE RECIPES

SALADS

SAVOURIES

SANDWICHES

HOT BREADS

PLUM PUDDING AND MINCE PIE

## RAGOUT OF TURNIPS

Put 2 tablespoons of butter in a saucepan, and when melted add 1 tablespoon of chopped onion and 4 cups of diced turnips, and stir until they begin to brown; season with 1 teaspoon of salt, 1 saltspoon of pepper, 1 teaspoon of sugar, and add slowly 1 cup of vegetable broth or milk into which 1 tablespoon of flour has been made smooth. Let simmer gently for half an hour.

## TELTOWER RÜBCHEN

Buy the imported "rübchen," which are the daintiest tiny turnips, and heat them in their own liquor; then drain and serve with Spanish sauce.

## PARISIAN TURNIPS

Cut turnips into small rounds with a Parisian potato cutter, and boil them for half an hour or until tender, the time depending largely upon the age of the turnips. Drain, and cover with highly seasoned white sauce, to which 1 tablespoon of chopped parsley has been added.

# VEGETABLE COMBINATIONS

## CHOP SUEY

Put 1 cup of onions, fried until brown, 1 cup of celery cut in two-inch pieces and then shredded and stewed in vegetable stock for half an hour, 1 cup of fried mushrooms, and 2 cups of boiled rice in a saucepan with a cup of thin brown sauce. Let all heat together for ten minutes, and season with salt and pepper.

## COLCANNON

This is made by the mixture of two or more vegetables already boiled. Use equal parts of mashed potato and sprouts (or any greens) finely minced, and grated onion if wanted, and add some mashed carrots or turnips or both; season with salt and pepper. Mix 2 eggs through 4 or 5 cups of vegetables, press into a mould, and boil or steam for half an hour. Turn out to serve, and serve plain or with a brown sauce.

## MACEDOINE OF VEGETABLES

Boil 1 small cauliflower and set it aside to drain; then boil 2 cups of diced carrots, drain them when tender, but reserve the stock. Add to the carrots the cauliflower carefully separated into little pieces, 2 cups of boiled peas, or 1 can, 1 cup of cooked or canned flageolets, ½ a cup of carrot stock, 1½ teaspoons of salt, 1 small saltspoon of pepper, and 1 tablespoon of sugar. Let simmer together until heated, and then add 1 chopped onion, 2 bay leaves, 1 tablespoon of butter. If liked, a sauce made of 1 tablespoon of butter and 1 tablespoon of flour thinned with the carrot stock and highly seasoned can be strained over the vegetables before serving.

## CANNED MACEDOINE OF VEGETABLES

Delicious combinations of peas, shaped carrots, flageolets, etc., can be had in bottles. Drain them, and put in a saucepan with 1 tablespoon of butter and some pepper and salt. When hot serve or add ½ cup of cream. Serve to garnish, or alone, or use to fill peppers, or tomatoes, or patties.

## VEGETABLE CHOWDER

Pare and slice in rather thick slices, enough potatoes to make 4 cups, and prepare the same amount of shredded cabbage, and sliced onions. Put 2 tablespoons of butter in a saucepan, and when melted add the onions, and cook them for ten minutes. Butter a large casserole, arrange over the bottom a layer of sliced potato, then a layer of cabbage, then one of onions, seasoning each with pepper and salt, and sprinkling with chopped hard-boiled egg, and so fill the dish. Pour 2 cups of milk, into which 1 tablespoon of flour has been made smooth, over the chowder, set the dish in a shallow pan of water, and bake slowly for one hour. If the milk cooks away add a little more during the cooking. The same dish can be made in a kettle, in which case halve the potatoes and cook for three quarters of an hour.

## VEGETABLE PIE (ST. GEORGE'S HOUSE)

Boil enough carrots, turnips, and large white haricot beans to make a ½ cup of each when chopped or sliced after cooling, and enough potatoes to make a scant cup when sliced. Slice enough Bermuda onions to make ½ cup, and fry in butter until golden brown; then mix the onions and prepared vegetables, and add to them ¼ cup each of canned peas, green beans, and tomatoes. Season well with salt and pepper, stir in 1 teaspoon of chopped parsley, dampen with the water in which the haricot beans cooked, heap into a deep baking dish, cover with a good crust, and bake until slightly browned.

## VEGETABLE HASH

Chop separately 5 medium-sized potatoes, 2 sweet green peppers (carefully seeded), 5 fresh tomatoes, 1 cup of boiled beets (½ a can), and 2 raw onions.

Put 2 tablespoons of butter in a frying pan, and when melted add the chopped onions, and let simmer slowly for five minutes, then add the tomatoes and let simmer another five minutes, then put in the potatoes, the peppers, and the beets. Dredge well with salt and pepper, and, stirring occasionally, let all cook slowly until the juices are nearly absorbed; then let the hash brown on the bottom, and turn out with the brown on top. Garnish with squares of toast.

## VEGETABLE STEW

Put 4 tablespoons of butter in a large saucepan, and when melted add to it ½ cup of sliced onions, ½ cup of diced carrots, 1 cup of shredded celery, and ¼ cup of turnips cut in oblong pieces, and toss them in the butter for fifteen minutes; then pour over them 6 cups of cold vegetable broth or water, add 1 teaspoon of salt, 2 bay leaves, 6 small onions halved, 4 carrots cut in quarters, 6 small squares of turnip, and let simmer slowly for half an hour; then add 5 potatoes cut in half, and let cook for half an hour more, and add more vegetable broth to keep the vegetables covered. Make dumplings, and drop into the boiling stew, cover tightly, and cook ten minutes more; season well with salt and pepper, and serve with enough of the stock, thickened with a little flour and butter, to cover.

## VEGETABLE CASSEROLE

In order that this dish should taste and appear at its best, it should be cooked and served in an Italian casserole dish from eight to ten inches in diameter. Peel 8 medium-sized onions, and take the layers off until a centre about three quarters of an inch in diameter is left; toss the centres in hot butter until browned, and chop the outside. Cut 3 medium-sized sweet green peppers in half, lengthwise, and fill each half liberally with a mixture of bread crumbs, chopped tomato, chopped onion, and salt and pepper. Stuff 6 solid, medium-sized tomatoes in any of the ways described under stuffed tomatoes. Put 2 tablespoons of butter in a saucepan, and when melted add to it 2 tablespoons of chopped onions; fry these for ten minutes, then stir in 2 tablespoons of flour, and use vegetable stock or milk, 2 cups of either, to make a sauce; add 1 bay leaf, and enough soup-browning to make a rich colour. Put the stuffed peppers in a casserole dish with the glazed onion hearts and the sauce, cover, and let cook for ten minutes; then arrange the stuffed tomatoes in the casserole, distribute among them ½ can of button mushrooms, halved, ½ can of flageolets or peas, and leave the cover off the dish, letting it cook for fifteen minutes very slowly. This casserole can be varied in many ways, using different filling for the peppers and tomatoes, and either truffles, string beans, or fresh mushrooms in the sauce, which should not be too thick.

## VEGETABLE RAGOUT

Prepare for boiling what will make 3 cups of turnip when cut in inch squares, 1½ cups of potatoes, and 1½ cups of carrots. Put the carrots into slightly salted and sweetened water, let boil for ten minutes, then add the turnips and potato, and cook for ten minutes more. Put 2 tablespoons of butter in a saucepan, and when melted add 2 tablespoons of chopped onion, and fry until slightly browned; then add 2 tablespoons of flour, stir until smooth, and pour slowly into this 2 cups of the stock in which the vegetables cooked; then add 2 teaspoons of sugar, 1 teaspoon of salt, ½ teaspoon of pepper; and the diced vegetables; cover, and let simmer slowly for half an hour, then add 1 tablespoon of chopped parsley, and serve.

## BORDEAUX PIE

Slice enough Spanish onions to fill a cup ¼ full, and fry them in butter until slightly browned. Boil carrots to equal ½ cup when diced, potatoes enough to fill a cup ¾ full, and peel 2 cups of mushrooms, and toss them in a little butter in a frying pan over a moderate fire for ten minutes; hard boil 4 eggs, and make 1 cup of white sauce. Cut the vegetables in small pieces, slice the eggs, add ¼ cup of canned peas (or fresh boiled ones), 1 teaspoon of chopped parsley, salt and pepper well, put in a little grated nutmeg and 1 teaspoon of lemon juice, and mix all carefully with the white sauce. Line a large baking dish (or small individual ones) with thin crust, fill with the mixture, cover the top with crust, and bake until slightly browned.

## NEW ORLEANS STEW

Slice 3 onions, and fry them in 1 large tablespoon of butter for five minutes; then add to them 3 chopped sweet green peppers, stir well, and let cook together another five minutes; then scrape the contents of the frying pan into a double boiler, add the corn cut from 3 ears of sweet corn (or ½ can of corn), and 3 sliced tomatoes, 1 cup of water, 1 teaspoon of salt, 1 teaspoon of sugar, and let all cook together for one hour; season afresh before serving.

## INDIAN CURRY

Put 2 tablespoons of butter in a frying pan, and add to it when melted 2 onions chopped fine, and let cook very slowly for fifteen minutes. Mix 1 tablespoon of curry powder, 1 tablespoon of sour apple, or tamarind-chutney chopped fine, 1 teaspoon of salt, and enough vegetable stock to make a paste. When the onions are browned add this paste, and after stirring well put in 1 cup of boiled haricot beans, 1 cup of halved boiled chestnuts, and 1 can of halved button mushrooms, and let all simmer together for ten minutes. Have ready some stock made by putting 2 tablespoons of desiccated cocoanut into a bowl and pouring over it 1 cup of boiling water, and use this to dampen the cooking vegetables; then add 1 cup of vegetable broth, and let cook ten minutes more. We westerners are fond of this served in this way with chutney, but in India they press it through a strainer and serve it as a purée, adding to it 2 well-beaten eggs. Encircle with rice in serving.

## CURRY OF LENTILS

Soak 2 or 3 cups of German or Egyptian lentils for two or three hours; drain them, and put them in boiling water, and let them cook for three quarters of an hour or until tender but not broken. Salt well when they have been cooking a short time, and when done drain them, sprinkle with salt, and heap in a pyramid on a round flat dish; garnish with 3 hard-boiled eggs cut in half, encircle with boiled rice, and pour curry sauce over the lentils only. Serve extra sauce in a sauce-boat and Indian chutney.

## CURRY OF SUCCOTASH

Heat 1 can of Lima beans and 1 can of sweet corn, and when hot drain, and heap on a flat dish; cover with curry sauce, and serve with potato croquettes and Indian chutney.

## CREOLE CURRY

Boil 1 cup of rice, and while it is cooking put 2 cups of okra, 2 cups of tomato, and 2 small onions cut in halves, and 1 teaspoon of butter in a double boiler, and when hot add 1 cup of hot water, into which has been dissolved 1 heaping teaspoon of curry powder, and let all cook together for half an hour; remove the onions, add the rice, season generously with salt, and serve with Indian chutney.

## VARIOUS VEGETABLE CURRIES

Almost any vegetable makes a good curry,—flageolets, carrots and peas, button mushrooms, etc., and either boiled rice or rice croquettes should be served. A garnish of Spanish pimentos looks well, and the curry sauce should be plentiful. Hard-boiled eggs halved are always nice with curry, and Indian chutney should be served with it.

# NUT DISHES

### ITALIAN CHESTNUTS

Chestnuts can be cooked either by roasting or by boiling. If roasted, the thin brown that clings to the nut is removed with the outer shell; if boiled, the inner skin often has to be removed with some trouble. Roast chestnuts by putting them in a hot oven for eight or ten minutes, then use a small, sharp knife and peel them from the point down.

To boil chestnuts put them, in their shells, in cold water and let them cook for five or six minutes after the water starts boiling, or put them in boiling water for ten or twelve minutes. Peel carefully, and serve after roasting or boiling with brown sauce or mushroom sauce, plain or in cases.

### CHESTNUT PURÉE

Roast or boil 6 cups of Italian chestnuts, remove the shell and inner skin and chop them fine or put them through a vegetable mill. Put them in a double boiler with milk enough to cover them and let them cook slowly for fifteen or twenty minutes, or until the milk is all absorbed. Stir frequently, add 1 tablespoon of butter, 1 tablespoon of cream, plenty of salt and a little pepper. The purée should be the consistency of mashed potato.

### PEANUT PURÉE

Shell 3 or 4 cups of peanuts, remove the inner skin, and put through a vegetable mill. Put in a double boiler with milk to cover them, season with salt, and let cook gently half an hour, or until tender. Stir frequently, and serve when the milk is absorbed and the peanut purée is the consistency of mashed potato. A tablespoon of whipped cream is an improvement if added during the last moments of cooking.

## MICHAELMAS LOAF

Mix 1 cup of finely ground walnuts (or other nuts), 1 cup of finely ground roasted peanuts, 1 teaspoon of salt, 1 saltspoon of pepper, 2½ cups of fine bread crumbs, 1 tablespoon of mixed sweet herbs (thyme, sage, and summer savory), and 1 large onion or 2 small ones chopped fine. When well blended bind together with 2 eggs which have been slightly beaten, mould with the hands into a loaf, place in a well buttered roasting tin, and let it cook for ten minutes in a moderately hot oven; then add 1 tablespoon of butter and 1 cup of hot water, and baste frequently during half an hour's cooking. The loaf should be well browned and carefully removed to a hot platter. Make a brown sauce in the pan in which the loaf cooked, and serve with this and cold apple sauce.

## NUT AND FRUIT LOAF

Chop mixed nuts enough to make 2 cups, and add to them 6 bananas chopped fine and ½ teaspoon of salt; mix well together, and press into a plain mould. Stand the mould in a steamer, and let it steam for three hours. Serve ice-cold, sliced, with pickles or catsup.

## CHRISTMAS LOAF

Make as in foregoing recipe, omitting the chopped onion and adding another half tablespoon (or even more) of the sweet herbs. Serve with cranberry sauce.

## ROAST NUT AND BARLEY LOAF

Make a brown sauce with 2 tablespoons of olive oil, ½ cup of browned flour, and use water or vegetable stock for thinning; chop 1 large onion fine, and fry it in 1 tablespoon of oil or butter, and mix the onion and the sauce with 2 cups of cold boiled pearl barley, 1 cup of finely ground roasted peanuts, 1 cup of fine bread crumbs, 1 teaspoon of salt, and 1 saltspoon of pepper. With the hands mould into a loaf, place in a roasting pan which has been well buttered, and let cook in the oven for ten minutes; then add 1 tablespoon of butter and 1 cup of hot water, and baste every five minutes for half an hour. Make a brown sauce in the same pan, or serve with Caper sauce. Garnish, if brown sauce is used, with English savoury croquettes.

## STEAMED NUT AND BARLEY LOAF

Make as in the foregoing recipe, but pack into a mould, set this in boiling water, and let it steam for an hour and a half or two hours. Let cool in the mould, and turn out to serve cold, or to slice, or to use for nut hash.

A brick-shaped mould will be made by any tinsmith to order, or the large sizes of baking-powder tins can be used to steam loaf.

## ROASTED NUT LOAF WITH HOMINY

Grind 2 cups of nuts,—pecans, walnuts, roasted peanuts, etc., or use peanuts only,—and mix with them 2 cups of cold boiled hominy, ½ cup of bread crumbs, 3 hard-boiled eggs chopped fine, 1 tablespoon of chopped parsley, 1 tablespoon of grated onion, and 1 raw egg. Form into 1 large roll, or several smaller ones, put in a buttered tin, and let bake in a quick oven for half an hour; baste with a little butter and water a few times. Garnish with slices of lemon, and serve with brown sauce. This loaf may be steamed as directed for barley loaf and used hot, cold, or in hash.

## FOUNDATION LOAF

This loaf can be made and kept in readiness for use, as it will remain fresh for several days if it is left in the covered mould in which it cooked and is kept in a cool place. Put 2 cups of water in a saucepan, and when the water boils stir into it 1 cup of a finely ground cereal, preferably gluten flour or meal, or Scotch oatmeal, and stir until thick; then add 2 teaspoons of salt, ½ teaspoon of pepper, 1 tablespoon of butter, and 1 cup of shelled peanuts which have been put through a vegetable grinder twice. Pack the mixture into a loaf-shaped mould, or large round tin with a tight-fitting lid, almost immerse it in water, and let it steam for two hours. Use when cold, either for nut hash or croquettes, or with an equal amount of bread crumbs and the seasoning to make Michaelmas or Christmas loaf.

## NUT HASH

Use cold steamed nut loaf and the same amount of cold boiled potatoes. Chop the potatoes and the loaf separately, and add to them, after mixing, ¼ as much chopped onion. Turn into a frying pan which contains melted butter well covering the bottom, dredge with salt and pepper, and stir frequently with a knife during the first ten minutes' slow cooking; then let the hash brown on the bottom, shaking the pan vigorously from time to time, season afresh, and turn out with the browned portion on top. One or 2 chopped green peppers can be added to the hash, if the flavour is liked.

# RICE, MACARONI, Etc.

## BOILED RICE

Wash 1 cup of rice by letting water run through it in a sieve, and put it in a large double boiler, the top of which contains plenty of water at boiling point; add 1 teaspoon of salt, and let it boil, tightly covered, for twenty-five minutes; pour off the water then from the rice, still holding the cover on, and again place it over the boiler, and let the rice steam for another twenty minutes, when it will be found that each grain is separate, as it should be. Use a fork to scrape it lightly into the serving dish.

## BAKED RICE

Let ½ cup of rice soak for several hours in 2 cups of warm water. Drain and put in a baking dish, and cover with 3 cups of milk containing ½ a teaspoon of salt. Cover the dish, and let bake slowly for an hour or until the milk is absorbed and the separate grains of rice are soft.

## INDIAN RICE

Put 1 tablespoon of butter into a double boiler, and when melted add 1 onion chopped fine, the juice from 1 can of tomatoes, 6 tablespoons of rice, 1 teaspoon of curry powder, some salt and pepper. Cover and let cook together for three quarters of an hour.

## SPANISH RICE

Put 2 tablespoons of butter in a saucepan, and when melted add ½ cup of rice, and stir it for fifteen minutes; then add 1 chopped onion, 1 chopped tomato, and 1 clove of garlic, cover with hot water or vegetable stock, and season highly with salt and pepper; stir well, then cover, and let the rice cook slowly for forty minutes.

## RICE-TOMATO STEW

Take 1 cup of cold boiled rice, and put with it in a saucepan 1 teaspoon of butter, 3 or 4 sliced tomatoes (or a cup of drained canned ones), 1 bay leaf, some celery salt, pepper and salt, and stir well together; let cook slowly for ten minutes, taking care that it does not burn; remove the bay leaf, and serve on thick slices of toast.

## FRIED RICE

Press newly boiled rice into an inch-deep pan, cover with a weight, and let it become cold. Cut into two-inch squares, and fry until brown in hot butter. Serve with tomato or curry sauce.

## ESCALLOPED RICE

Butter a baking dish, and sprinkle the bottom with a layer of boiled rice, and cover this with slices of hard-boiled eggs; dot well with butter, sprinkle with salt and pepper, then arrange another layer of rice and egg, etc., alternating thus until the dish is filled. Cover the top with bread crumbs, pour over all 2 tablespoons of melted butter, moisten with ½ cup of milk, and bake slowly for twenty minutes.

## RICE AND CHEESE

Butter a baking dish well, and sprinkle a half-inch layer of boiled rice on the bottom; season with salt and pepper, and dot well with butter; then arrange a generous layer of grated cheese, and sprinkle this with English mustard mixed with water, then add another layer of rice, and so continue until the dish is well filled, having the rice on top. Pour over all ½ cup of milk, or of the water in which the rice boiled, and let cook slowly in the oven for twenty minutes.

## BAKED RICE AND TOMATOES

Butter a baking dish well, and put a layer of rice in the bottom of it, and over this arrange slices of tomatoes; dot well with butter, and season plentifully with pepper and salt and celery salt, then place another layer of rice, and so proceed until the dish is well filled. Pour ½ cup of canned tomato juice over the rice, sprinkle the top with grated cheese, and bake for twenty minutes.

## ITALIAN RICE

Put 1 tablespoon of butter in a saucepan, and when melted add to it 2 cups of boiled rice and 1 cup of tomato sauce or tomato chutney; season well with salt and pepper, stir until heated through, and serve plentifully sprinkled with grated cheese.

## RICE AU GRATIN

Put 1 cup of milk in a double boiler, when hot add to it 1 tablespoon of flour mixed with 1 tablespoon of butter, 1 teaspoon of grated onion (or a few drops of onion extract), and ½ teaspoon of salt; stir into this 2 cups of boiled rice, let cook for five minutes, then put in a buttered baking dish, with ½ cup of grated cheese on top, dredge this with paprika, sprinkle with bread crumbs, and let brown in the oven.

## RICE OMELET

Beat the yolks and whites of 2 eggs separately, and to the yolks add ¼ of a cup of milk, ⅓ of a cup of cold boiled rice, 1 tablespoon of melted butter, some salt and pepper, and finally the stiff whites of the eggs. Put in a buttered omelet pan, and proceed as in making the usual omelet, cooking over a slow fire and shaking the pan vigorously. Sprinkle with salt and a little paprika; when set, turn together; serve with a sauce if desired, and garnish with watercress.

## RICE CZARINA

Butter a baking dish, and put an inch-deep layer of boiled rice in the bottom. Over this sprinkle finely chopped fresh or canned tomatoes, season with salt and pepper, and dot well with butter; then place another layer of rice somewhat thinner, and over this spread finely chopped green peppers, and so alternate tomatoes, peppers, and rice until the dish is well filled, having a layer of rice on the top. Garnish this with thin slices of tomato in the centre, and encircle the edge with thinly cut rings from the peppers. Pour 2 tablespoons of melted butter over all, cover lightly with a tin cover, and let cook in a slow oven for twenty minutes; just before serving add 2 more tablespoons of melted butter.

## SAVOURY RICE

Butter a baking dish, and half fill it with freshly boiled rice, sprinkle this with salt, pepper, celery salt, and a few drops of Worcestershire Sauce, then dot with mustard mixed with water, and pour ½ cup of tomato sauce over the surface evenly. Fill the dish with the remaining rice, and season again with the same ingredients, adding ½ cup of grated cheese (sage cheese preferably); after pouring on the tomato sauce cover with a thin layer of crumbs and bake fifteen minutes in a slow oven.

## UNPOLISHED RICE

Unpolished rice is used extensively in rice-growing countries, and has a quite distinct taste. When it can be obtained it makes a pleasant change, and can be served in any of the ways described for rice.

## PEARL BARLEY

Pearl barley should be put in plenty of boiling water and cooked for an hour, then drained, and prepared in any of the ways described for the serving of rice.

## AMERICAN MACARONI

Break ¼ of a package of macaroni into two-inch lengths, and drop it into rapidly boiling salted water. Let it boil for twenty-five minutes, then drain, and arrange with alternate layers of grated cheese in a buttered baking dish. Season each layer with pepper and salt, and when the dish is filled pour over all 1 cup of hot milk into which 1 tablespoon of flour and 1 of butter have been made smooth. Cover the top with crumbs and bake twenty minutes or until browned.

Some makers of macaroni recommend putting the macaroni in cold water for fifteen minutes after boiling it, and then reheating it with seasoning, etc.

## MACARONI AU GRATIN

Break ¼ of a package of macaroni into two-inch lengths, and put it into 2 quarts of rapidly boiling salted water; let boil rapidly for twenty-five minutes, then drain. Butter a baking dish, and put in it a half-inch layer of the macaroni, sprinkle generously with grated cheese, and season with salt and pepper; then put another layer of macaroni, and proceed as before until the dish is well filled, having macaroni on the top. Dot evenly with butter, and bake about fifteen minutes or until a golden brown.

## MACARONI BIANCA

Break half a package of macaroni into two-inch lengths, and drop it slowly into 2 quarts of rapidly boiling salted water; in fifteen minutes pour off all but 1 cup of the water, and add ½ cup of hot milk, stir often with a fork, and let boil until nearly dry or until tender, which will be in ten or fifteen minutes, and lift the macaroni into a strainer the instant it is cooked. Butter a baking dish, and put in it a layer of macaroni, dredge with salt and pepper, then sprinkle lightly with a layer of grated cheese (using 1 cup for the whole dish); dot well with mixed mustard, and sprinkle with Worcestershire sauce. Fill the dish with layers in this way, pour ½ cup of milk over all, and bake fifteen or twenty minutes, or until brown, in a quick oven.

## ITALIAN MACARONI

Break ¼ of a pound of macaroni into four-inch lengths, put in boiling salted water, and let it cook for twenty-five minutes. Drain, and put in a saucepan with 1 tablespoon of melted butter and 1½ cups of tomato sauce; season well with salt and pepper, and serve on a hot flat dish with grated cheese plentifully sprinkled over it.

## MACARONI WITH TOMATO AND ONION SAUCE

Boil ¼ of a package of macaroni in rapidly boiling salted water for twenty-five minutes, and whilst it is cooking prepare a sauce as follows: Put a large tablespoon of butter in a saucepan, and when melted stir into it 1 minced onion, 1 tablespoon of chopped parsley, and season with salt and pepper. Let cook together for six or seven minutes, then add 1 tablespoon of flour and 1 cup of stewed and strained tomatoes, and stir well together for five minutes. Butter a baking dish, put a layer of macaroni in it, then a layer of sauce, and so on till the dish is well filled, and set in the oven for ten minutes before serving.

## BAKED MACARONI ITALIAN

Boil ¼ of a pound of macaroni broken in two-inch lengths for twenty-five minutes, then drain, and put it in a buttered baking dish with 1 cup of tomato sauce; season well with salt and pepper, and put a half-inch layer of grated cheese on the top, and bake for fifteen minutes.

## MEXICAN MACARONI

Put 1 tablespoon of butter in a saucepan, and when melted stir into it ½ a can of tomatoes, 1 small sweet green pepper, seeded and chopped fine, 1 large onion chopped fine, and ½ teaspoon of salt. Cover, and let cook very slowly for about forty minutes. Then press through a coarse sieve, and put in a double boiler to keep hot. Boil ¼ of a package of macaroni for twenty-five minutes, drain, and pour over it the hot sauce.

## PLAIN MACARONI AND CHEESE

Put ¼ of a package of macaroni into boiling water, and let cook twenty-five minutes; drain, add 1 cup of hot milk, 1 tablespoon of butter, salt, pepper, and paprika; let boil up once, add ½ cup of grated cheese, and let cook five minutes more before serving.

MACARONI RAREBIT

Put in a saucepan 2 tablespoons of butter, and when melted add 1 cup of grated cheese and stir until the cheese is melted, and then add ½ a teaspoon of salt, ½ a teaspoon of mustard, ½ teaspoon of paprika, and 1 tablespoon of flour dissolved in ½ cup of cream (or milk), to which also add 3 slightly beaten eggs; mix all together thoroughly, put in 1 cup of cooked macaroni, and serve with toast.

SPAGHETTI

Spaghetti can be cooked in any of the ways described for macaroni, but real Neapolitan spaghetti is cooked as follows:—Break 1 lb. of spaghetti into 3 or 4 inch lengths, and put in a large saucepan full of highly salted boiling water and let boil for half an hour. At the same time put 1 cup of good olive oil in a frying pan and when hot put in it 2 green peppers, seeded and chopped, and let simmer until they begin to brown, then add 4 to 6 cloves of garlic cut fine, and 4 large tomatoes, peeled, quartered, and thinly sliced. Let cook for about half an hour or until the oil is all absorbed, and stir often. When cooked to the consistency of a thick sauce, sprinkle with salt and paprika; drain the spaghetti thoroughly, mix the sauce through it and serve on a large platter, sprinkling with freshly grated Parmesan cheese.

NOODLES

To make noodles add ½ cup of sifted flour containing ¼ of a teaspoon of salt to 1 large egg which has been slightly beaten. Mix well with a fork, and when stiff enough work with the fingers until the dough becomes very smooth and about the consistency of putty, and then wrap in a cloth and lay aside for half an hour. Sprinkle a bread-board well with flour, and roll the dough out upon this five or six times, rolling it thinner each time; at the last roll it as thin as possible without breaking, then roll it lightly together like a jelly-cake roll, and with a very sharp knife, beginning at one end, cut it into slices about ⅛ of an inch wide if to be used for soup, and ⅜ of an inch wide if to be used with a sauce. With the fingers shake these ribbons until they are separated, and let them dry for about half an hour.

Cut about ⅕ of the noodles very fine, and when dried, drop these in hot oil and fry until crisp and brown; serve these sprinkled over the boiled noodles.

To boil noodles, drop them in rapidly boiling salted water, cover them, and let them boil for twenty minutes, and then drain thoroughly.

Boiled noodles are delicious served with any brown sauce or tomato sauce, and can be used as directed for macaroni or spaghetti.

Very good noodles can be bought already made.

## GERMAN NOODLES

Put 2 cups of dried noodles into boiling salted water, let them cook rapidly for twenty minutes, drain, and put in a saucepan with 1 tablespoon of butter and 1 cup of brown sauce, to which has been added 1 tablespoon of reduced vinegar and a few capers if liked. Serve when thoroughly heated through, and add a little salt and pepper when in the dish.

## ITALIAN NOODLES

Put 2 cups of dried noodles into boiling salted water, let cook twenty minutes, drain, and put in a saucepan with 1 tablespoon of butter and 1 cup of tomato sauce or chutney. Season with pepper and salt, and serve on a hot dish, with the top well sprinkled with grated cheese.

# CROQUETTES

### BEAN CROQUETTES

Wash 2 cups of dried beans, then soak them in water for twelve hours or more, and cook in the same water about an hour or until tender; strain off the water, press through a sieve, and add 1 teaspoon of salt, 1 saltspoon of pepper, 1 tablespoon of butter. Stir well together, shape into croquettes, dip in beaten egg and crumbs, and fry in deep vegetable fat. Serve with tomato or horse-radish sauce.

### CHEESE CROQUETTES

Beat the white of 1 egg very stiff, and stir into it 1 cup of fine bread crumbs, 1 cup of grated cheese, ½ teaspoon of salt, and 1 saltspoon of paprika. Shape into balls or croquette forms, then roll in the beaten yolk of egg and crumbs, put in a frying basket, and fry in boiling vegetable fat until a golden brown. Lay on brown paper in the oven for three minutes, then arrange in a heap on a paper doily, dust with grated cheese, and garnish with watercress or parsley.

### SWISS CHEESE CROQUETTES

Melt 3 tablespoons of butter, add a few drops of onion juice, ¼ cup of flour, ½ cup of milk, the yolks of 2 eggs, 1 cup of grated American cheese, and ½ cup of Swiss cheese cut into small pieces. Let cook in a double boiler until the cheese is melted, then season with salt and cayenne; let cool, then shape into croquettes, roll in crumbs, and fry in deep fat.

## CHESTNUT CROQUETTES

Peel, blanch, and chop fine enough Italian chestnuts to make 2 cups, and boil them in water or milk to cover them for three quarters of an hour or until they are tender and the milk absorbed; let cool somewhat, then add 1 cup of bread crumbs, and 1 beaten egg, and ½ teaspoon of salt. Shape into croquettes, roll in egg and crumbs, and fry in deep fat. Serve with mushroom sauce or as a garnish.

## EGG CROQUETTES

Hard boil 10 or 12 eggs, add to them 1 tablespoon of chopped parsley, chop very fine, and season highly; then moisten with milk or cream. Mould into shape, roll in egg and crumbs, and fry in hot fat. Serve as a garnish to rice or tomatoes, or as a separate dish alone, or with curry sauce, horse-radish sauce, tomato sauce, or devilled sauce.

## FARINA CROQUETTES

Put 2 cups of milk in a double boiler, and when hot add 1 cup of farina and some salt. Cook until well thickened, and then whip vigorously into it 1 beaten egg. Let cool, mould into croquettes, dip in crumbs, and fry in hot fat. Serve with savoury sauce or with jelly melted to the consistency of cream.

## HOMINY CROQUETTES

Put 1 pint of cooked hominy into a saucepan, add 2 tablespoons of cream or milk, and stir over the fire until hot, then remove from the fire and season with salt; add the yolks of 2 eggs lightly beaten, shape into croquettes, roll in crumbs, and fry until nicely browned. Serve with some savoury sauce or as a garnish to scrambled or fried eggs.

## LENTIL CROQUETTES

Put 1 cup of well-washed lentils into 3 cups of water or vegetable broth when at boiling point, and let them cook slowly for an hour or until tender, strain them, and mash them in water, and let them cool.

Put 1 tablespoon of butter in a saucepan, and when melted add 1 finely chopped onion, and let cook for ten minutes; add this to the lentils, with 2 slices of bread which have been well soaked in milk, 2 beaten eggs, and enough fine bread crumbs to make the mixture thick enough to form into croquettes. Season highly with salt and pepper, shape into form, roll in egg, and then in crumbs, put in a frying basket, and fry in deep fat. Serve with horse-radish or onion sauce.

Lentil croquettes may also be served with caper sauce, and each croquette garnished with a slice of seeded lemon.


## MACARONI CROQUETTES

Have ready a kettle of salted boiling water, then shake into it ½ cup of macaroni, and let boil briskly for half an hour; then drain, and cut into small pieces. While the macaroni is cooking, make a sauce of 1 cup of hot milk to which is added 1 tablespoon of butter and 2 tablespoons of flour rubbed together, to which add, when thickened, the yolks of 2 eggs well beaten, 1 teaspoon of salt, 1 saltspoon of pepper, and the chopped macaroni (the sauce must not cook after the eggs are added). Turn out to cool, and when cold form into pyramid-shaped croquettes, roll in egg and crumbs, and fry in deep fat. Serve with tomato sauce and a little sprinkling of grated cheese.

## ITALIAN CROQUETTES

Put 1 tablespoon of butter in a saucepan, and when melted add 1 finely chopped onion, let cook slowly for five minutes, then add 2 cups of boiled macaroni, 1 cup of milk, cover, and stirring frequently let simmer slowly for half an hour or until the milk is absorbed; add 1 cup of drained canned tomatoes, or 2 or 3 chopped fresh ones, and 1 tablespoon of grated cheese, 1 teaspoon of mixed mustard, 1 tablespoon of highly flavoured catsup, salt and pepper. Cook for ten minutes more, then add ½ cup of bread crumbs and 2 teaspoons of chopped parsley. Turn into a bowl, and when somewhat cooled add 1 beaten egg and stir it well through the mixture. When cool and firm form into shapes, brush with egg, roll in crumbs, and fry a golden brown in deep fat. Serve plain or with tomato or curry sauce.

## TOMATO CROQUETTES

Take ¾ of a cup of stewed tomatoes without any juice, put in a saucepan over the fire, and stir into them 1 tablespoon of butter, 1 cup of mashed potatoes, ½ cup of grated bread crumbs, and some salt and pepper. Mix well together, and then add 1 lightly beaten egg. Remove from the fire, turn into a deep plate, and when cold form into croquettes; dip each in egg and bread crumbs, fry until brown, and serve with a savoury sauce.

## DRIED PEA CROQUETTES

Put 1 cup of dried peas in cold water or broth, let cook for 1½ hours or until tender, then strain and mash. Add to them 1 finely minced onion which has been fried ten minutes in 1 tablespoon of butter, salt, pepper, 2 tablespoons of flour, 2 eggs, and bread crumbs to make stiff enough to shape into croquettes or flat cakes. Roll in crumbs, and fry golden brown in deep fat. Serve with onion or tomato or mint sauce.

## NUT CROQUETTES WITH POTATO

Chop or grind 2 cups of mixed nuts, and mix with them 2 cups of mashed potatoes, 1 teaspoon of grated onion, 1 teaspoon of salt, 1 dash of nutmeg, and 2 yolks of raw eggs. Shape into croquettes, dip in egg, and crumbs, and fry in hot, deep vegetable fat.

## NUT CROQUETTES WITH SALSIFY

Use ½ cup each of ground pecans and walnuts, and with them mix 2 cups of boiled mashed salsify, 1 teaspoon of salt, 1 tablespoon of grated onion, 1 tablespoon of chopped parsley, 2 tablespoons of bread crumbs, form into croquettes, roll in egg and crumbs and fry in deep fat. Serve with tomato chutney.

## NUT CROQUETTES WITH COCOANUT

Grind 1 cup of any sort of nuts, and add to them 2 cups of bread crumbs, ½ cup of grated cocoanut, 4 tablespoons of peanut butter, ½ teaspoon of celery seed, 1 teaspoon of salt, and 1 egg, well beaten. Mix well, and form into croquettes or balls, dip in egg and crumbs, and fry in deep vegetable fat.

Nut croquettes can be made of the mixtures given for nut loaf, rolled in egg and crumbs and fried.

## POTATO CROQUETTES

Take 2 cups of mashed potatoes and stir into them 2 lightly beaten eggs, ½ teaspoon of salt, and a little paprika, and 1 tablespoon of chopped chives or parsley; form into croquettes or rolls, roll in egg and fine crumbs, and fry in deep fat.

## POTATO CROQUETTES WITH CHEESE

To 2 cups of cold mashed potatoes add the beaten yolk of 1 egg, 1 tablespoon of grated cheese, 1 tablespoon of milk or cream, and a few drops of onion extract; season with pepper and salt, form into shapes and fry in deep fat.

## SAVOURY POTATO CROQUETTES

To 2 cups of cold mashed potatoes add 1 beaten egg, 1 chopped onion, 1 tablespoon of chopped parsley, 1 tablespoon of mixed sweet herbs, and 1 tablespoon of cream. Shape, roll in egg and fine crumbs, and fry in deep fat.

## MASHED POTATO CROQUETTES WITH PEAS

To 2 cups of cold mashed potatoes add 1 egg, pepper and salt, and form into flat, small cakes; in the centre of each put 1 teaspoon of canned peas, then lap the potato mixture over these, and form into balls. Dip in egg and crumbs and fry in deep fat.

## CREOLE POTATO CROQUETTES

To 2 cups of mashed potatoes add 1 beaten egg, pepper and salt, and 2 tablespoons of chopped green peppers (or chopped red pimentos) which have been fried in butter for ten minutes; shape, roll in egg and crumbs, and fry in deep fat.

## SWEET POTATO CROQUETTES

To 2 cups of mashed sweet potato add 1 beaten egg, pepper and salt; shape and roll in egg and crumbs, and fry in deep fat.

## SWEETENED RICE CROQUETTES

Soak 1 cup of rice three hours in warm water, then drain and put into a double boiler with 1 pint of boiling milk, and let cook for half an hour; then add 1 tablespoon of sugar, 1 tablespoon of melted butter, and ½ teaspoon of salt, and let simmer ten minutes more. Let cool somewhat, and then stir in slowly 3 eggs, which have been beaten to a froth, and stir until it thickens; then add the grated peel of 1 lemon, and turn out upon a dish to cool. When cold and quite stiff form into balls or oval croquettes, dip in very fine cracker crumbs, and fry in deep fat. Serve alone with sauce or as a garnish.


## CAROLINA CROQUETTES

Boil eggs ten minutes, remove the shells, press the yolks through a sieve or potato-ricer, chop the whites fine, and mix with the same amount of boiled rice; dampen with a little melted butter, season with pepper and salt, form into balls, roll in egg and crumbs, and fry in deep fat. When a golden brown drain and serve with some savoury hot sauce, or as a garnish to curry.


## PLAIN RICE CROQUETTES

Mix together 2 cups of cold boiled rice, ½ teaspoon of salt, and 1 tablespoon of melted butter, 1 tablespoon of flour, and 1 beaten egg. Form into balls, roll in flour, and fry in deep fat. Serve while crisp.


## PINK RICE CROQUETTES

Make croquettes as above, but omit the sugar and add ¼ teaspoon of paprika and 2 tablespoons of tomato catsup to the rice before frying.

## CURRIED RICE CROQUETTES

Put ¾ of a cup of milk in a saucepan with butter the size of an egg and let it boil; then stir into it 1 cup of rice that has boiled twenty minutes in salted water. Add 1 small teaspoon of curry powder, a few drops of onion juice, and salt to taste. When the milk boils remove from the fire and add a beaten egg to it, stirring vigorously. Let cool, shape into croquettes, and fry in hot fat. Serve apple sauce or onion sauce with these croquettes.

## ENGLISH SAVOURY CROQUETTES

To each cup of fine bread crumbs use 1 tablespoon of mixed sweet herbs and 1 teaspoon of minced onions and bind all together with 1 egg, slightly beaten. Season with ½ teaspoon of salt, 1 scant saltspoon of pepper, ½ teaspoon of celery salt, form into balls, roll in egg, and then in crumbs, and fry in deep fat until golden brown. Serve with a brown sauce or as a garnish to nut loaf.

## MIXED VEGETABLE CROQUETTES

Boil separately ten carrots and 3 turnips and 5 potatoes and chop fine; then mash, and add to them 1 tablespoon of butter and 3 tablespoons of hot milk. Put 1 tablespoon of butter in a frying pan, and when melted cook slowly in it for ten minutes, or until beginning to brown, 1 large onion chopped fine. Add this to the mashed vegetables, also 1 tablespoon of chopped parsley, and season with salt and pepper. When cool form them into croquettes or flat cakes, and dip in egg, and then in fine crumbs, and fry. If croquettes are made fry in deep, hot fat; if cakes are made they can be fried in a frying pan like pancakes, and browned on one side, then on the other. Serve plain, or as a garnish to other vegetables, or with Spanish sauce.

Any of the mixtures for croquettes can be moulded into flat cakes and fried until browned in butter on a griddle or in a shallow frying pan.

# TIMBALES AND PATTIES

EGG TIMBALES

Into 1 cup of milk rub 1 heaping tablespoon of flour until smoothed, add 1 tablespoon (measured before melting) of butter, the lightly beaten yolks of 4 eggs, ½ teaspoon of salt, 1 saltspoon of pepper, and the same amount of celery salt. Beat the whites of the eggs until very stiff, and stir these into the other ingredients with a fork. Turn into buttered timbale moulds, and set these in a pan containing hot water which almost reaches the top of the moulds. Let bake in a moderate oven for fifteen or twenty minutes or until well set. Turn out on a hot, flat dish and serve with tomato sauce or bread sauce.

SAVOURY EGG TIMBALES

Make the foregoing recipe, but add 1 tablespoon of chopped onion and 1 tablespoon of chopped parsley, or substitute minced shallots, chives, or onion tops.

EGG-TOMATO TIMBALES

Make plain egg timbales, but instead of using milk use 1 cup of tomato juice from canned tomatoes. Add 1 tablespoon of chopped parsley, or chives if desired.

PEA TIMBALES

Take 1½ cups of boiled peas, put them through a ricer, or mash to a pulp, and when cooled add to this 2 lightly beaten eggs, 1 teaspoon of chopped mint, 1 teaspoon of grated onion (or chopped chives), 2 tablespoons of melted butter, ½ teaspoon of salt, and 1 saltspoon of pepper. Fill timbale moulds, set in a pan containing some hot water, and cook in a moderate oven fifteen or twenty minutes or until well set. Turn out and serve with sauce.

## CORN TIMBALES

Take 1 cup of canned corn and add to it 4 eggs slightly beaten, ½ teaspoon of salt, a little paprika, ½ teaspoon of onion juice, ½ teaspoon of sugar, and 1¼ cups of milk. Pour into buttered timbale moulds, or a large mould, and set in hot water, and bake in the oven about twenty minutes or until firm. Turn out and garnish with slices of broiled tomatoes.

## POTATO AND CHEESE TIMBALES

Take 6 or 7 good-sized potatoes, boil and mash them, and beat into them 4 tablespoons of butter and 2 eggs; then add 1 cup of grated cheese, 1 teaspoon of salt, and some paprika, press into small moulds or cups, and let cook as directed above for about twenty minutes. Turn from the moulds, and serve with a sauce of melted butter to which is added a little grated cheese, paprika, and chopped parsley.

## POTATO TIMBALES

Beat 3 eggs (yolks and whites together), add to them ¼ of a cup of cream, then 2 cups of mashed potatoes, 1 teaspoon of grated onion, a little pepper, 1 teaspoon of salt, and some nutmeg; beat together until perfectly smooth, and then press into timbale moulds, the bottoms of which are covered with buttered paper. Stand these in a shallow pan containing boiling water in the oven, and let cook for about twenty minutes. Then loosen the sides with a thin knife, and turn out carefully onto a heated flat dish. Garnish with peas or macedoine vegetables, or use as a garnish.

## RICE TIMBALES

To 1 cup of boiled rice add 1 chopped hard-boiled egg, 1 tablespoon of tomato catsup, ½ teaspoon of salt, 1 saltspoon of pepper, 2 tablespoons of melted butter, and 2 well-beaten eggs. Fill well-buttered timbale moulds with this mixture, set them in a pan containing warm water, and bake in a slow oven for twenty minutes, or until well set.

Timbale cases, pastry cases, ramekins, or patties may be filled with any of the following recipes and served as a separate course at luncheon or dinner.

## ARTICHOKE PATTIES

Boil Jerusalem artichokes as directed, cut in half-inch cubes, cover with a highly seasoned white sauce, and use to fill patties or cases.

## ASPARAGUS PATTIES

Use only the tender ends of white or green canned asparagus, heat in white sauce, and use to fill cases or patties.

## CELERY PATTIES

Use celery prepared as in creamed celery, only cut the stalks into inch-long pieces. Fill heated pastry cups or patties with the mixture.

## CHESTNUTS IN CASES

Peel 2 cups of Italian chestnuts, and blanch them by pouring boiling water on them and letting them stay in it until the skins remove easily; then cut them in quarters, put them in boiling water, and boil them half an hour or until soft. While they are finishing cooking put 1 tablespoon of butter in a saucepan, and let it cook slowly until a rich dark brown then add to it 1 tablespoon of flour, and stir until as smooth as it will come, then add 1½ cups of milk and 1 teaspoon of caramel or soup-browning, and season highly with salt and pepper. Put the chestnuts in the sauce, and fill pastry cases with the mixture.

## PATTIES OF FRESH GREEN PEAS

Use fresh green peas boiled as directed, or use canned French peas; reheat in white sauce, and use to fill patties or timbale cases. A little finely chopped mint can be added to the sauce if liked.

## EGG PATTIES

Hard boil the eggs required, chop fine when cold, and reheat in parsley sauce, and use to fill heated cases or patties, or use eggs Newburg for filling.

## MACEDOINE PATTIES

Use imported macedoine of vegetables, heat in a double boiler with white sauce, and use as patty filling in heated cases.

## MUSHROOM PATTIES

Cut fresh mushrooms in quarters, toss them in melted butter for five minutes, then cover them with white or brown sauce, and serve in heated cases or patties. Any of the recipes given for mushrooms can be used to fill patty cases, mushrooms Newburg being especially suitable.

### CANNED MUSHROOM PATTIES

Toss the mushroom buttons in hot butter for five minutes, cover them with white sauce, and use to fill heated patties.

# SAUCES

### CARAMEL FOR COLOURING

Put ½ cup of powdered sugar in a small saucepan over a very low fire, stir with a wooden spoon until melted, and continue to stir until it is a rich brown; add 2 cups of *warm* water, and let it simmer for fifteen or twenty minutes, then skim and strain, and bottle for use in giving a rich colour to soups and sauces.

Ready-made vegetable extracts of good dark colour can be bought, and are one of the few things which seem better than the home-made product.

### REDUCED VINEGAR

This adds a delicious flavour to many sauces, vegetables, and soups, and is made by putting vinegar, with a little salt and pepper, in a saucepan and letting it boil rapidly until reduced, the proportions being 2 tablespoons of vinegar, 1 saltspoon of salt, and a pinch of pepper cooked until reduced to 1 teaspoon of liquid. Strain before using.

### SAUCE BERNAISE

Into 1 tablespoon of reduced vinegar beat slowly the yolks of 4 eggs to which has been added 2 tablespoons of cold water, and when well mixed hold in a small saucepan above a slow fire; put in a small bit of butter, and when melted stir in another, and so continue until 1½ tablespoons have been used. When the sauce is smooth and creamy, season with salt and pepper or paprika, and add ½ teaspoon of tarragon vinegar, or 1 teaspoon of minced tarragon leaves. The sauce cannot be served very hot or it will curdle. It may be served cold also.

## BLACK BUTTER SAUCE

Put 3 or 4 tablespoons of butter in a saucepan with 1 saltspoon of salt and a little pepper, and let cook slowly until browned; then add 1 teaspoon of reduced vinegar or lemon juice, and serve hot.

## BREAD SAUCE

Put 1 large slice of bread, cut an inch thick, into 2 cups of milk with 1 onion with 4 cloves stuck in it, add pepper, salt, and 1 teaspoon of butter. Let simmer until the bread is quite soft, lift out the onion and cloves, beat well with a fork, and serve. Serve fine golden brown bread crumbs with the sauce, as these belong with it.

## BROWN SAUCE

Put 1 tablespoon of butter in a saucepan, and when well browned, remove from fire, add 1 tablespoon of flour, stirring until smooth; then add gradually 1 cup of vegetable stock or milk, and, when all is smooth and well thickened, ½ teaspoon of brown colouring, and salt and pepper. It improves the flavour to let the stock to be used simmer for ten minutes with 1 bay leaf and ½ an onion added to it.

## VARIATIONS OF BROWN SAUCE

Add chopped button mushrooms, chopped fried peppers, tiny pearl onions, boiled eggs, etc., to vary brown sauce.

## SAUCE BORDELAISE

To 1 cup of brown sauce add 1 teaspoon of grated onion, 3 minced fresh mushrooms (or 1 tablespoon of chopped canned ones), 2 teaspoons of chopped parsley, and salt and pepper. Stir over a slow fire for five minutes before serving.

## DRAWN BUTTER

Melt 4 tablespoons of butter, and stir in until smooth 2 tablespoons of flour; then add slowly 2 cups of boiling vegetable stock, 1 teaspoon of salt, and a little cayenne or paprika.

## CURRY SAUCE

Put 1 tablespoon of butter in a saucepan, and when melted stir into it 1 large onion chopped fine, and let simmer for six or seven minutes; then add 1 sour apple chopped fine (or, if it can be had, 1 tablespoon of tamarind chutney), stir for three or four minutes, then add ½ cup of strong vegetable stock or water, and let cook gently for five minutes; pour on another ½ cup of vegetable stock and 1 cup of milk, into which 1 dessert spoon of curry powder has been stirred until smooth; let all boil up once, then press through a sieve, pressing well to get the juices, return to the fire, and to thicken, use 1 tablespoon of flour blended with 1 tablespoon of butter to every cup of liquid. Stir until the consistency of thick cream, and add a little salt before serving. The quantity of curry powder here named will make a mild curry sauce.

## CAPER SAUCE

Put 1 tablespoon of butter in a frying pan, and when melted add 1 tablespoon of flour and stir until smooth. Now add, a little at a time, 2 cups of vegetable broth, and stir until it boils and is smooth. Put in 2 heaping tablespoons of capers and 1 chopped hard-boiled egg, and season well with salt and pepper. One tablespoon of cream may be added at the last to enrich the sauce if desired.

## CHEESE SAUCE

Make 1 cup of highly seasoned white sauce, and add to it 1 scant cup of grated cheese; stir in a double boiler until the cheese is melted, then add a few drops of yellow colouring extract, and salt and paprika.

## FRENCH CUCUMBER SAUCE

Grate 1 cucumber and drain it well, then add to it ½ teaspoon of salt, a dash of cayenne, and 1 tablespoon of vinegar.

## DUTCH BUTTER

To every tablespoon of melted butter add 1 teaspoon of lemon juice; season with salt.

## DEVILLED SAUCE

Put 1 tablespoon of butter in a saucepan, and when melted add 1 tablespoon of chopped onion, and let cook slowly for five minutes. Then add 1 tablespoon of chopped parsley, 2 tablespoons of vinegar, 1 tablespoon of walnut or mushroom catsup, 1 tablespoon of English mustard, ½ teaspoon of salt, 1 saltspoon of black pepper, and a little cayenne. Thicken with 1 tablespoon of flour, and when smooth add enough vegetable stock to make the consistency of cream. The sauce may be used as it is or pressed through a sieve to strain.

## FRENCH SAUCE

Rub together 1 tablespoon of flour and 1 of butter, and put in a saucepan; as it melts add slowly 1 cup of boiling water or vegetable stock, let boil, stirring constantly, then remove from the fire, and when somewhat cooled add the juice of 1 lemon, 2 tablespoons of tarragon or chervil vinegar, 2 egg-yolks slightly beaten, and salt and pepper.

## GERMAN SAUCE

Make brown sauce, add ½ can halved button mushrooms and 1 tablespoon of reduced vinegar, and season with salt and pepper.

## GERMAN EGG SAUCE

Mix 3 beaten egg-yolks with 1 teaspoon of flour, 1 scant cup of cream or milk, 1 tablespoon of butter, and 1 tablespoon of lemon juice, season with salt and pepper, and beat vigorously, until thickened, over a hot fire, but do not let the sauce boil at all. Add 1 hard-boiled egg, chopped fine, and 1 tablespoon of minced parsley before serving.

## EGG SAUCE

To 1 cup of well-made white sauce add 2 hard-boiled eggs chopped fine, and 1 teaspoon of chopped parsley, and a little salt and paprika.

## HERB SAUCES

Make a good white sauce and to each 2 cups of sauce add the herbs selected, prepared as follows: Take a handful of the leaves, and after washing them well put them in a pan with a little salted boiling water; let cook for five minutes, then drain, and dry with a cloth, and put in a mortar with 1 tablespoon of butter, and macerate until fine; add this to the white sauce. In this way parsley, mint, tarragon, chervil, and other herb sauces can be made.

## SAUCE HOLLANDAISE

To 1 tablespoon of reduced vinegar add the yolks of 4 eggs mixed with 2 tablespoons of cold water; stir well together, and cook by holding above a very slow fire, in order to prevent curdling; add 2 tablespoons of butter, stirring it in a little at a time until all is used. Season with salt and pepper and serve warm or cold.

## HORSE-RADISH SAUCE

Rub together 1 tablespoon of butter and 1 of flour and put in a saucepan. When melted and smooth from stirring, add slowly 1½ cups of heated milk; when properly thickened by slow cooking, put in 3 tablespoons of grated horse-radish, stir well, season with salt, add 1 teaspoon of butter, and serve on croquettes, etc.

## MAÎTRE D'HÔTEL SAUCE

This is made by using sauce Hollandaise and adding to it 1 tablespoon of lemon juice and 1 tablespoon of finely chopped parsley.

MINT SAUCE

Wash the mint and take ½ cup of the leaves; chop them fine, macerate in a mortar, then cover with 1 cup of hot vinegar, add 1 teaspoon of sugar, and let stand a few moments before using.


MUSHROOM SAUCE

Make brown sauce and add to it ½ can of button mushrooms, halved. Let heat through before serving.


NUT SAUCES

For these use pignola (pine) nuts, almonds, chestnuts, or any other sort. Remove the shells, blanch in boiling water to remove the inner skin, and chop them very fine. Put 1 tablespoon of butter in a frying pan, and when melted add to it 1 tablespoon of chopped onion, and let cook for five minutes; then add ½ cup of chopped nuts and stir until brown, scrape the contents of the pan into a mortar, and pound them well. Blend 1 tablespoon of flour and 1 tablespoon of butter, put in a saucepan, and when melted and smooth add ½ cup of milk and ½ of the nuts; let cook slowly two or three minutes, add another ½ cup of milk and the remaining nuts. Salt well, and add a little pepper; let cook very slowly, and when the sauce is the proper thickness stir in 1 tablespoon of thick cream.

The sauce can be darkened with brown colouring, or by browning the thickening flour in butter.

## ONION SAUCE

Chop 4 onions very fine and brown them in 3 tablespoons of butter; add 1 tablespoon of flour, let this brown also, and thin with 1 cup of broth or water or milk. Add pepper and salt, and beat 1 egg-yolk into it before serving. Serve either strained or unstrained.

## PARSLEY BUTTER

Put butter in a saucepan, and when melted add finely chopped parsley and some salt, using 1 teaspoon of parsley to every tablespoon of butter used. Serve on boiled potatoes, asparagus, etc.

## PARSLEY SAUCE

Into 2 cups of white sauce stir 1 beaten egg and 2 tablespoons of finely chopped parsley.

## SAUCE PROVENÇAL

To 1 cup of Spanish sauce add 1 tablespoon of white wine, 2 tablespoons of tomato sauce, and 1 tablespoon of chopped chives, and cook together slowly ten minutes before serving. Season with salt and pepper before serving.

## PIQUANT SAUCE

Put 4 tablespoons of vinegar in a saucepan with 1 tablespoon of chopped shallots or onions, and let cook slowly until only 1 tablespoon remains; add to this 1 cup of Spanish sauce, and when at boiling point put in the sauce 2 teaspoons of minced sour pickles, 1 teaspoon of chopped parsley, and some salt and pepper; serve with croquettes or vegetables.

## SAUCE RAVIGOTE

Ravigote is merely the name applied to the mixture of herbs combined with flavouring for this sauce. These are chives, cress, burnet and chervil, in equal proportions. Use 2 tablespoons of the mixed herbs, scald them in tarragon vinegar, drain them, chop them fine, and add them to 1 cup of plain mayonnaise.

## SAUCE ROBERT

This is made by adding to 1 cup of Spanish sauce 2 tablespoons of white wine, 1 teaspoon of onion juice, and 1½ teaspoons of mustard mixed with 2 teaspoons tarragon vinegar. Season, and make hot in a double boiler, letting all cook slowly together ten minutes.

## SPANISH SAUCE

This is a rich sauce which is used as a basis for many sauces, and can be made at a leisure time and used any time within a few days. Any stock in which vegetables have been cooked may be used, but the best one is made as follows: Wash 4 or 5 cups of red beans or lentils, and after soaking them in 2 quarts of water for ten hours or more empty them with the same water into a saucepan, and put with them 3 onions halved, 3 sprigs of parsley, 1 cup of carrots quartered, ½ cup of diced turnips, 1 tablespoon of salt, 2 stalks of celery cut in short lengths, and a small bag containing 1 teaspoon of thyme, 2 bay leaves, 6 cloves, 6 whole peppers, and 1 teaspoon of allspice berries. Let boil hard for one minute, then set on the stove where it will simmer slowly for two hours. Strain the broth through a fine sieve, and use the vegetables in a stew, a deep pie, or a curry. To finish the Spanish sauce put 2 tablespoons of butter in a saucepan, and when melted stir into it 2 tablespoons of flour and let brown, stirring constantly; then add a little stock at a time until about 2 cups have been used and the sauce is the consistency of thick cream. Darken with 1 teaspoon of brown colouring, add 1 tablespoon of sherry, and pepper and salt.

SPINACH SAUCE

Put 1 cup of freshly cooked or canned spinach, from which the juice has been pressed, into a basin or mortar, and chop or mash to a pulp. Melt 1 tablespoon of butter in a saucepan, add to it 1 small onion chopped fine, let cook slowly for five minutes, then add the spinach, and let cook for ten minutes more. Put 1 cup of milk into a double boiler with 1 bay leaf, 1 stalk of celery (or some celery seed), and when it boils add 1 tablespoon of flour blended with 1 tablespoon of butter; season with salt and pepper, and when thickened stir the spinach into this, sprinkle with grated nutmeg, and let cook together for ten minutes. Press through a sieve before serving.

SAUCE TARTARE

Make a plain mayonnaise sauce (see Salads), and to each cup add 1 teaspoon of gherkins and 2 teaspoons of capers, both very finely minced; sprinkle a little cayenne on the sauce before serving.

TOMATO SAUCE

Use 6 fresh tomatoes, and after washing them slice them, skins and all. Put 1 tablespoon of butter in a saucepan, and when melted add 2 tablespoons of finely chopped onion, let cook slowly for five minutes, then put with them the tomatoes, 2 bay leaves, 1 clove of garlic, 1 teaspoon of sugar, some pepper and salt, and let cook gently for fifteen minutes; then strain, pressing through a sieve, and return the liquid to the fire to simmer until reduced to the proper consistency.

## TOMATO SAUCE WITH OTHER VEGETABLES

Make tomato sauce, using with it chopped celery, chopped peppers, or chopped mushrooms, which have been fried for ten minutes in hot butter and added after the sauce is strained.

## WHITE SAUCE

Put 2 tablespoons of butter in a saucepan, and as soon as it is melted stir into it slowly 3 tablespoons of flour, using 1 tablespoon at a time, then add slowly 2 cups of warm vegetable stock or milk, stirring all the while; then add ⅔ of a teaspoon of salt, 1 saltspoon of pepper, and cook slowly for five minutes, stirring constantly; add 1 tablespoon of butter, and stir for another minute. Some flour thickens more than others, and if the sauce seems too thick, thin with a little cream or milk.

White sauce may be varied in many ways by using onion juice, mushroom catsup, chopped chives, etc.

The white sauce may be made in a double boiler. Put the milk in the top receptacle, and when boiling add the flour dissolved in a little cold milk, then the butter, etc., and let cook ten minutes or until thickened.

## SAUCE VINAIGRETTE

To each cup of French dressing add 1 tablespoon of minced onion and 1 tablespoon of macerated parsley.

### TOMATO SAUCE WITH NUTS

Chop 2 tablespoons of blanched nuts, fry them for ten minutes in 1 tablespoon of melted butter, and add these to strained tomato sauce.

### TOMATO SAUCE WITH EGG

To each cup of strained tomato sauce add 2 hard-boiled eggs chopped fine.

# EGG DISHES

### BOILED EGGS

Eggs are very palatable when put in boiling water and cooked for three or three and a half minutes, but some cooks recommend that "boiled eggs" should never boil, but instead, be placed in a large saucepan which is filled with water that has boiled and just been removed from the fire. The instructions are to cover the saucepan closely after putting the eggs in the water, and let it stand on the back of the stove, the eggs to be removed in ten minutes if wanted soft, and in twenty minutes if liked well set. Hard-boiled eggs are certainly more palatable cooked in this way than when boiled for ten minutes in the ordinary way.

### FRIED EGGS

Put a little butter into a small frying pan, and when melted break an egg into a saucer, and slide it carefully into the hot butter, and let it fry until the white is thoroughly set, cooking as many as are required, separately, in the same way. If a tight cover is put over the frying pan when the egg is put in, the yolk of the egg will be as pink as a nicely poached egg when done. Season with pepper and salt before serving. A little Worcestershire sauce or walnut catsup heated in the pan and poured over fried eggs adds variety.

## POACHED EGGS

Fill a deep frying pan ⅔ full of hot water, and stir into it one teaspoon of vinegar and 1 teaspoon of salt. When the water reaches boiling point break the eggs carefully one by one into it, remove the pan from the intense heat, cover it, and let the eggs cook until the whites are firmly set. If the water is shallow the eggs will spread and be more flat, in which case the boiling water must be dipped up over the yolks with a spoon to make them pink; if the water is deep the eggs will be more round than flat. When the eggs are done lift them carefully from the water with a perforated strainer in order to drain off the water thoroughly, and serve them on hot toast.

## POACHED EGGS WITH GRAVY

Poach eggs and serve them with Sauce Bernaise, or any piquant sauce.

## POACHED EGGS INDIENNE

Poach the number of eggs required, and after placing them on toast pour over them a thin curry sauce.

## EGGS WALDORF

Place nicely poached eggs on toast, and fit a freshly cooked mushroom as a cap over each yolk. Surround the toast with brown sauce containing quartered mushrooms.

## SCRAMBLED EGGS

Break six or more into a bowl, beat them lightly with a fork, and pour them into a frying pan into which 1 tablespoon of butter has been melted; stir continually over a very slow fire until they are well set, seasoning them meanwhile with pepper and salt, and adding another ½ tablespoon of butter in small pieces during the cooking. Serve with a garnish of small triangular pieces of toast. One tablespoon of cream can be added to the eggs before serving if desired. Eggs may be scrambled with milk, using ½ cup of milk to 4 eggs, and then proceeding as above.

## SCRAMBLED EGGS WITH CHEESE

Make plain scrambled eggs, and when nearly set add 2 tablespoons of grated cheese for every 6 eggs used, and 1 tablespoon of chopped parsley. Serve on toast.

## SCRAMBLED EGGS WITH MUSHROOMS, PEAS, ETC.

Scramble 6 eggs, and two or three minutes before removing from the fire add to them a can of button mushrooms cut in slices, lengthwise, and 1 tablespoon of finely chopped parsley. In the same way peas, tomatoes, asparagus tips, chopped sweet peppers, etc., can be used.

## SAVOURY SCRAMBLED EGGS

Prepare plain scrambled eggs, and just before taking off the fire add 2 tablespoons of chopped chives (or green stems of young onions or shallots can be used instead), and ½ a tablespoon of finely chopped parsley; serve on hot toast.

## SCRAMBLED EGGS INDIENNE

Make plain scrambled eggs, and just before serving stir into them 1 tablespoon of cream, into which has been stirred 1 teaspoon of curry powder and ½ teaspoon of onion juice. Serve on hot toast.

## SPANISH EGGS

For 6 eggs use 1 large tomato and 1 small onion. Chop the onion fine, and fry it five minutes in 1 tablespoon of butter; then add the chopped tomato, and stir another minute over the fire. Now pour in the eggs and scramble them, adding 1 teaspoon of salt and a saltspoon of pepper. Garnish with small triangles of toast.

## SHIRRED EGGS

Butter individual gratin dishes, and break into them 1 or 2 eggs as desired. Season with salt and pepper, and a sprinkling of finely chopped parsley, and put into the oven for five minutes, or until the eggs are set. Place each dish on a small plate with a paper doily.

## SHIRRED EGGS WITH TOMATOES

Use as many shallow, individual gratin dishes as there are persons to be served, and, after buttering each dish, break into it 1 egg, taking care not to break the yolk. Halve some small tomatoes, and set one half, cut side up, in each dish; season the whole with pepper and salt, and set in the oven for ten minutes or less.

## GRIDDLED EGGS

Heat a griddle and butter it slightly, and break upon it 3 or 4 eggs, disturbing the yolks so as to break them. When a little browned on one side turn them with a cake-turner and fry the other side.

## PLAIN OMELET

Put 3 or 4 eggs in a bowl and beat them ten or twelve times with a fork vigorously. Put 1 scant tablespoon of butter in a frying pan, and as soon as melted turn in the eggs and shake over a slow fire until they are set; season with salt and pepper, turn the omelet together as it is let to slide from the pan, and place on a hot dish. Make several small omelets rather than one large one, and place on white paper doilies, and garnish with parsley to serve. The trick of shaking an omelet is the secret of making a good one, and the egg mixture should be not over ½ an inch deep in the pan.

## OMELET SOUFFLÉ

Take 4 to 6 fresh eggs, separate the yolks and whites, and beat each until as light as possible. Butter a deep frying pan, mix the yolks and whites lightly together with a fork, and put in the hot frying pan, smoothing somewhat with a fork to level. Season the top with pepper and salt, and shake over a slow fire until the omelet is delicately browned on the bottom; turn it together and serve on a hot platter.

## HERB OMELET

Make like plain omelet, stirring with every 4 eggs used 1 teaspoon each of powdered thyme, or sweet marjoram, sage, chopped onion tops or chives, and parsley.

## CHEESE OMELET

For omelet soufflé made with 6 eggs add ¼ cup of grated cheese to the yolks of the eggs, and ¼ cup to the beaten whites before putting them together.

In making plain omelet with cheese add ¼ cup of cheese to 4 eggs after they are in the omelet pan. Sprinkle with grated cheese to serve, and garnish with watercress or parsley.

## RUM OMELET

Make an omelet soufflé, put on a hot dish, and pour ½ cup of heated rum around it, and light it with a match. Rum is easily made to blaze if a teaspoon is filled with it and a lighted match held under the tip of the spoon. The rum on the platter can then be easily lighted with that in the spoon.

## BAKED OMELET SOUFFLÉ

Beat the whites of 6 eggs very stiff and the yolks of 3. Mix the whites and the yolks, using a fork; then stir in the juice of half a lemon and 3 tablespoons of powdered sugar. Heap in a buttered baking dish, and cook in a hot oven about fifteen minutes.

## EGGS CARMELITE

Prepare 1 cup of very finely chopped boiled spinach by adding to it 1 teaspoon of butter and 1 saltspoon of grated nutmeg, and put where it will keep warm. Hard boil 6 or 8 eggs, then cut each carefully in two, lengthwise; remove the yolks and stir them into the spinach, mashing them well, and mashing all together until the yolks are thoroughly mixed with the spinach; then season with salt and pepper and neatly fill the halves of the whites of the eggs with the spinach. Make a sauce with 2 cups of milk, 1 teaspoon of butter, and 2 tablespoons of flour, a dash of paprika, and 1 cup of grated cheese. When this has thickened arrange 2 or 3 halved eggs in each individual gratin dish, and pour around them some of the sauce, and set in the oven five minutes to make thoroughly hot, or serve on a large dish garnished with small triangular pieces of toast.

## EGG WITH MASHED POTATO

Use a long, narrow gratin dish, and arrange cold mashed potato in it in ridges with a spoon, and make three or four hollows in the surface. Into each of these break an egg, and let all bake in the oven until the eggs are set. Tomato or white sauce can be served with this.

## EGGS NEWBURG

Hard boil 6 eggs, plunge them into cold water for a moment, then peel, and when cooled, so they will not crumble in cutting, cut them in half. Have ready a sauce made of 1 cup of cream (or milk) and 3 tablespoons of butter, to which when hot is added 2 tablespoons of sherry, 2 tablespoons of brandy (the latter may be omitted), 1 saltspoon of pepper, and 1 teaspoon of salt. Let cook three minutes, then beat in vigorously the beaten yolks of 4 eggs, stir until thickened, add a dash of paprika, and serve over the hard-boiled eggs on toast.

## EGGS LYONNAISE

Put 2 tablespoons of butter in a frying pan, and when melted add 1 finely chopped onion, and let simmer slowly for eight or ten minutes; then add 1 tablespoon of flour, and stir well until smooth. Add to this ½ cup of milk, ½ teaspoon of salt, and ½ saltspoon of pepper, and let cook three or four minutes only. Pour into a deep gratin dish, and break upon it 6 eggs; sprinkle with ½ cup of bread crumbs, and let cook in a moderate oven about five minutes, or until the eggs are set. Serve in the same dish.

## JAPANESE EGGS

Hard boil the number of eggs required, and, after halving them, remove the yolks, and mix them with a little butter (using 1 tablespoon to 6 eggs), pepper, salt, and a little tomato chutney or Harvey sauce. Refill the halved whites with this, and use the eggs to garnish 2 cups of boiled rice. Pour over all 1 cup of white sauce or parsley sauce to serve.

## GOLDEN ROD EGGS

Hard boil 5 eggs, take off the shell, and separate the yolks from the whites, chopping the whites fine and pressing the yolks through a sieve, keeping whites and yolks separate. Put 1 cup of milk in a double boiler, and when it boils add to it 1 tablespoon of butter and 1 tablespoon of cornstarch which have been rubbed together, and when the sauce has thickened season it generously with pepper and salt, and stir into it the chopped whites of the eggs. While the sauce is cooking prepare 5 rounds of toast, and place them on a hot dish. Cover each piece of toast with a layer of white sauce, sprinkle this with a layer of the yolks, then more of the white sauce, and the remainder of the yolks, season with salt and pepper, and stand in the oven a moment or two before serving.

## FROTHED EGGS

Separate the yolks and whites of as many eggs as are required, putting each yolk in its shell or in a separate dish. Beat the whites until very stiff, and fill a well-buttered custard cup half full of the white of egg; make a hole in the centre, sprinkle with salt, pepper, and lemon juice, and drop a yolk in each cup. Put in a shallow pan of boiling water with a cover on it, and when the eggs are set turn out onto buttered toast. Garnish with parsley butter.

## FRIED STUFFED EGGS

Hard boil 6 eggs and halve them carefully, removing the yolks. Put the yolks through a sieve, and rub to a paste with 1 tablespoon of melted butter, salt, pepper, and ¼ cup of cream or milk, using a little at a time, so as not to use it all unless needed to make the mixture of the right consistency for refilling the halved whites. Carefully fill the places made vacant by the removed yolks, roll the half-egg in beaten egg and crumbs, and fry in deep, hot fat. Serve with 2 cups of white sauce, and add to it 2 tablespoons of diced pickled beets, which makes the sauce pink.

This same effect may be had to some extent by simply using hard-boiled eggs, frying them, and serving with same sauce or white sauce, to which 1 tablespoon of capers has been added.

## SWISS EGG TOAST

Melt 1 tablespoon of butter on a shallow or flat dish, and sprinkle over it 1½ tablespoons of grated cheese; then break into the butter 3 eggs, taking care not to break the yolks. Sprinkle well with salt and pepper and 1½ tablespoons of grated cheese mixed with 2 teaspoons of finely chopped parsley. Bake in the oven until the eggs are set, then cut each egg out round with a cutter, and serve on rounds of toast.

## DEVILLED EGGS

Hard boil the number of eggs required, halve them, and serve on toast with devilled sauce.

## EGGS CAROLINA

To serve four persons hard boil 6 eggs, then put them in cold water for one minute, peel 2 of them, chop the whites, and mix with melted butter and 1 tablespoon of chopped parsley, and form into nests on 4 pieces of hot "corn bread." Then peel the other 4 eggs, and arrange one on end in each nest. Pour a little parsley butter on each, and season with salt and pepper.

## MÜNCHNER EGGS

Hard boil 6 eggs, then peel them, and put each on a leaf of lettuce or cabbage, encircling it with grated horse-radish, and serve with a sauce made of vinegar to which is added salt and dry mustard.

## EGGS IN MARINADE

Hard boil the eggs required, then remove the shells, and stick 4 cloves in each egg. Put 2 cups of vinegar on to boil, and rub together a little vinegar, ½ teaspoon of mustard, ½ teaspoon of salt, and ½ teaspoon of pepper, and stir into the boiling vinegar. Place the eggs in a glass jar, and pour the boiled vinegar over them. They can be used in a fortnight, halved or sliced as a garnish or in salads.

## EGGS PARISIENNE

Butter as many timbale moulds as are required, and dust the inside with chopped parsley; then break into each an egg, and sprinkle with salt and pepper. Set the moulds in water in a shallow pan, and place in the oven until well set or hard. Turn out onto a flat dish, or on individual dishes, and with them serve bread sauce, or any sauce desired.

## EGGS PERIGORD

Butter small moulds or cups, then sprinkle them with chopped parsley, and on the bottom (which will be the top when they are turned out) place a symmetrical pattern made of cut beets and truffles or pickled walnuts. Drop one egg into each mould, dredge with salt and pepper, and set the moulds in a pan of boiling water; cover, and let cook until firm. Turn out onto rounds of toast, and serve with a hot tomato sauce, or any savoury sauce.

## EGGS WITH CHEESE

Into a shallow round or oval gratin dish, or small individual dishes, put melted butter to cover the bottom, and encircle the outer edge with thinly sliced, rather dry, cheese; inside this break enough eggs to cover the bottom of the dish, taking care not to break the yolks. Season with salt and pepper, and put into the oven until the whites of the eggs are thoroughly set.

## EGGS MORNAY

Drop eggs into a buttered baking dish, and then cover them with a highly seasoned white sauce to which some egg-yolks have been added (using 1 yolk to each ½ cup of sauce), also salt and paprika. Sprinkle the top with grated cheese, and put in the oven to bake until the egg is firmly set.

## CREAMED EGGS

Butter a shallow dish, pour into it 1 scant cup of milk, and let heat. When hot cover the surface with eggs, cover, and let poach on top of stove until set; sprinkle with celery salt, and then cover with cream, and set in the oven for five minutes. Sprinkle the top with finely chopped celery tops to serve. This may be cooked in one large dish or in individual gratin dishes.

## EGGS OMAR PASHA

Butter individual gratin dishes, and break 2 eggs into each, taking care not to break the yolks. Slice small onions so the separate rings are unbroken, and place a circle of these rings on the eggs around the edge of the dish. Sprinkle with salt and pepper, then with grated cheese, and bake in a slow oven until the eggs are thoroughly set.

## TURKISH EGGS

Butter one large gratin dish or several small ones, break into them enough eggs to cover the bottom, taking care not to break the yolks; put them in a moderate oven until the whites are quite set, and then garnish by putting a few tablespoons of boiled rice on the eggs around the edge of the dish, alternating with button mushrooms, which have been cut in thin slices and mixed with brown sauce. Season with salt and pepper just before serving.

## EGGS BEURRE-NOIR

These are best served in individual gratin dishes measuring about four inches across. Put 2 tablespoons of butter in a saucepan, and let it cook over a slow fire until a rich brown, but not burnt. Add to it 1 teaspoon of lemon juice, and cover the bottom of each gratin dish with the (black) butter; then break into each dish 1 egg, or 2 if required, taking care not to break the yolk. Season with salt and pepper and arrange 8 or 10 capers on each; put in the oven eight or ten minutes, or until the eggs are well set. Set each dish on a doily on a small plate before serving, with a sprig of parsley on the side.

# EGGS CREOLE

Take a shallow gratin dish large enough to contain the eggs required, allowing 2 eggs to each person, butter the gratin dish, and break the eggs carefully into it, taking care not to break the yolks; season with pepper and salt, and set in a moderate oven until the whites are stiff; while they are cooking prepare the following garnish which will be sufficient for 6 or 8 eggs. Put 1 tablespoon of butter in a saucepan; when melted add 1 onion cut into thin slices, and stir it about three or four minutes. Then add to it 1 tomato which has been peeled and chopped, 1 sweet green pepper cut in very thin slices, each broken in several pieces, and ½ can of button mushrooms, which are prepared by draining and washing and cutting lengthwise in 3 or 4 pieces. Let all cook slowly together for eight or ten minutes, stirring carefully and adding more butter if necessary. When nearly cooked season generously with pepper and salt, add 1 tablespoon of tomato sauce, and when the eggs are removed from the oven place this garnish on the eggs, encircling the outer edge. This garnish can be varied as to quantities to suit taste, using more or less tomatoes or onions. This is very nice done in individual gratin dishes, 2 eggs being used in each dish.

# EGGS IN SAVOURY BUTTER

Savoury butter is made by melting good butter, and adding to it any chopped herb,—chives, parsley, etc. Put a little of this in individual gratin dishes, and break into them 1 or 2 eggs as desired. Pour a little of the savoury butter over the top of each egg, season with salt and pepper, and put in the oven until the eggs are thoroughly set. If fresh tarragon is available, two nicely shaped leaves crossed on the yolk of the egg make a pretty garnish, or two leaves of lemon verbena may be used instead.

## EGG MOULD FOR VEGETABLES

Make egg mixture as for egg timbales, and pour into a buttered ring mould. Cook in pan of water in the oven twenty minutes or until set, and then turn out onto a hot, round, flat dish, and fill the centre with hot button mushrooms which are mixed with tomato sauce, or with peas, either with or without the sauce.

## CANUCK EGG TOAST

Sprinkle fresh toast with walnut, mushroom, or any savoury catsup, then heap on it nicely scrambled eggs in which milk has been used, and on top put a generous layer of grated cheese; season with pepper and salt, and put under the oven flame of a gas stove. Let the cheese brown, then remove and garnish the top with slices cut from black pickled walnuts, or a few capers, or with thin strips of pimentos, or chopped chives.

## ESCALLOPED EGGS

Hard boil 8 eggs, cut the whites into medium-sized pieces, and press the yolks through a sieve or ricer. Put 1 cup of milk in a double boiler, and with it 1 tablespoon of finely minced onion, shallot, or chives. When the milk boils add to it 1 tablespoon of thickening flour dissolved in a little milk and stir until thickened. Season with ½ teaspoon of salt, ¼ teaspoon of pepper, a dash of paprika, and stir in the riced egg-yolks and the diced whites. Serve in small dishes, or covered with crumbs and browned in the oven, or on rounds of toast. One or 2 sweet green peppers finely chopped vary this dish.

# CHEESE RECIPES

### CHEESE RAMEKINS

Take 1 cup of bread crumbs and 1 cup of milk, and cook together until smooth; then add 2 tablespoons of melted butter, 1 scant teaspoon of mustard, and 6 tablespoons of grated cheese. Stir over the fire for one minute, then remove, and add salt and cayenne pepper, and the lightly beaten yolks of 2 eggs; afterwards stir in with a fork the whites of the eggs, beaten to a stiff froth. Pour into ramekin dishes, and bake for fifteen minutes in a moderate oven, or cook and serve in a baking dish.

### BAKED CHEESE AND BREAD

Soak 1 cup of bread crumbs for two or three minutes in 2 cups of milk, then beat in the yolks of 2 eggs thoroughly beaten, and 1 cup of grated cheese, and lastly the whites of the 2 eggs beaten to a stiff froth. Put into a buttered baking dish, dot the top with butter, sprinkle with bread crumbs, and bake until a light brown, which will be in from twenty minutes to half an hour.

### CHEESE FONDU

Put 1 tablespoon of butter in a saucepan, and when melted add 1 cup of milk, or cream if desired, 1 cup of fine bread crumbs, 2 cups of grated cheese, ½ teaspoon of salt, ½ teaspoon of dry mustard, and some cayenne pepper. Stir constantly until well heated through, and then add 2 lightly beaten eggs, and serve on rounds of toast.

## CHEESE RELISH

Put 1 cup of milk into a double boiler, season with pepper and salt, and when hot stir in 1 cup of grated cheese, and let cook for five minutes; then add 3 crumbed soda crackers and serve on toast, with a sprinkling of paprika.

## CHEESE MÉRINGUES

Beat the whites of 2 eggs to a stiff froth, and stir into them with a fork 2 tablespoons of Parmesan or grated cheese, 2 drops of tabasco, a little salt and paprika; drop 1 tablespoon at a time into hot fat, and fry until brown; then drain and sprinkle with fresh salt and paprika before serving.

## CREAMED CHEESE

Make 2 cups of well-seasoned white sauce, add a few drops of golden yellow colouring, stir into it ½ cup of cheese cut into dice (or grated if preferred), and when the cheese is softened and hot serve on rounds of toast and sprinkle with paprika.

## CHEESE PANCAKES

Make small pancakes of 1 cup of milk, 1 egg, and enough flour to thicken, and spread them with grated cheese moistened with a little melted butter; sprinkle chopped chives mixed with parsley over the cheese, and a dash of any savoury catsup (if liked), season with salt and pepper, roll the pancakes after cooking, and serve as a savoury or luncheon dish.

## COTTAGE CHEESE

Take 2 quarts or more of sour milk or cream, and add to it the same quantity of rapidly boiling water, turn into a straining-bag, and hang up until dry. When ready to use, turn out of the bag and rub until smooth; add a seasoning of salt and pepper and a little sweet cream. Beat until light and serve ice-cold. A little cream can be served to eat upon it, if liked.

This can also be made by heating the sour milk or cream and using no water, but the milk must only be heated enough to separate and not enough to boil.

## WELSH RAREBIT

Cut in very small thin pieces 1 pound of American cheese; put it in a chafing-dish and stir until melted, then add 1 teaspoon of mustard, some salt, and slowly stir in ½ a glass of beer or ale, and season with cayenne or paprika just before serving on toast.

## BACHELOR'S RAREBIT

Make Welsh rarebit, and five minutes before serving stir into it 1 tablespoon of chopped green peppers and 1 tablespoon of chopped Spanish pimentos.

## DELMONICO RAREBIT

Cut in small pieces 1 pound of American cheese, put it in a chafing-dish and stir until melted; then add ½ a glass of beer or ale, some salt and cayenne or paprika, 1 teaspoon dry mustard, the yolk of 1 egg, then the whipped white of the egg, and serve at once on toast. The white of the egg militates against any "stringiness" which is apt to come from cooking certain sorts of cheese. A little milk can be used, if desired, instead of beer.

## PINK RAREBIT

Drain 1 can of tomatoes and put them in a saucepan with 1 tablespoon of butter; season them well with pepper and salt, and after they have cooked fifteen or twenty minutes add 1 pound of fresh American cheese cut into thin slices, and stir until melted; season generously with salt and pepper, and serve on rounds of toast.

## LIPTAUER CHEESE

Remove the paper from the smallest Neufchâtel cream cheese, which is nearer like real Liptauer than any other that can be had in America, and set it in the centre of a plate; surround it with 1 teaspoon of paprika, ½ teaspoon of salt, a small mustard spoon of French mustard, a piece of fresh butter half the size of the cheese, 2 teaspoons of minced onion, and 1 teaspoon of capers. The "Liptauer" should be blended at the table with a silver knife. Add first the butter, then the capers, then the onion, then the seasoning, and make into a cream. Serve on brown or white bread, or crackers.

## ROQUEFORT CHEESE GOURMET

Cream ½ pound of Roquefort cheese with 1 tablespoon of butter and some salt and 1 tablespoon of sherry, and serve on water crackers.

## CAMEMBERT CHEESE

A pretty way to serve Camembert cheese is to place the cheese, when removed from its box and paper, on a round paper doily on a large plate, and surround it with a heavy wreath of watercress and radishes cut to look like flowers.

## CHEESE "DREAMS"

Cut fresh cheese into thin slices, spread with made mustard, sprinkle with paprika, lay between two trimmed slices of bread, and toast on both sides until nicely browned, using a very slow fire.

## GRATED CHEESE

Instead of throwing away bits of dried cheese these should be grated and put in a wide mouthed, covered glass jar.

# SALADS

There is no end to the combinations of vegetables for salads; the few here given are the best ones I have tried. The dressing should never be put on a fresh green salad until just as it is to be used; other salads, like potato, beans, etc., are sometimes improved by standing. Lettuce for salads should be carefully looked over; and clean, inner leaves not washed unless they are muddy; but all the leaves used which are washed should be thoroughly dried before adding the dressing. In France the salad basket is one of the most used kitchen utensils, and the salad leaves after washing are shaken in this until absolutely dry. The dressing should be very well mixed with the vegetables, and a little dry salt and pepper added as the salad is served.

# FRENCH DRESSING

An absolute rule for making good salad dressing is an almost impossible thing, as this seems to be the one place in cookery where it is not only allowable but commendable to "guess" at proper proportions. The following is as nearly accurate as it seems well to be. Put 1 scant teaspoon of salt and 1 saltspoon of black pepper in a bowl, and stir into them with a wooden fork, very slowly, 3 or 4 tablespoons of fresh oil, and then add half as much or less vinegar, mixing it well with the oil.

# TARRAGON VINEGAR

Good tarragon vinegar can be bought in any city, but it is so easily prepared at home that it is worth doing. Put a handful of tarragon in a quart jar, and cover with cold or heated vinegar. Seal the jar and set it in a dark place for a month or so before using.

Make chervil vinegar in the same way.

# PLAIN MAYONNAISE DRESSING

Put 2 chilled egg-yolks in a cold soup plate, and stir into them 1 teaspoon of salt and ½ teaspoon of mustard, using a silvered spoon, and after these are well mixed in begin to add oil, actually drop by drop, from 1 scant cup of cool olive oil, and do this until the eggs are so thickened that it is not possible to make them more so; then the remaining oil may be added less slowly. If this first process is not properly done, no amount of stirring will ever thicken the sauce. A fork or whisk may be used to finish the stirring. When the oil is added, beat in slowly 1 tablespoon of vinegar, and 1 of lemon juice, and ½ saltspoon of cayenne pepper. Put on the ice until wanted.

Tarragon mayonnaise is made by substituting tarragon vinegar for plain vinegar.

## GREEN COLOURING FOR MAYONNAISE

This may be made of mixed herbs or spinach. If herbs are used take 1 tablespoon of parsley, 1 of watercress, and 1 of chervil, put them into boiling water, let them cook eight minutes, then drain and pound in a mortar, and press the pulp through a fine sieve. Use this with mayonnaise to make a light delicate green colour.

If spinach is used press 1 tablespoon of chopped spinach through a sieve, and use it to colour the sauce.

## SALAD CHEESE BALLS

Use equal quantities of Neufchâtel cheese and grated American (or Parmesan) cheese, sprinkle with cayenne, and dampen with a little melted butter. Shape into tiny balls and use very cold as a salad garnish.

## AMERICAN SALAD

Use 1 cup of scraped thinly sliced celery, 1 cup of diced apples, ½ cup of chopped English walnuts, and ½ cup of seeded white grapes. Mix well with mayonnaise, and serve on large curled lettuce leaves.

## ARTICHOKE SALAD

Use cold boiled fresh artichokes, remove the thistles, and fill the artichokes with finely minced chopped onion, apple, and beet, blended with green mayonnaise; serve extra mayonnaise in which to dip the artichoke leaves.

### WAX BEAN SALAD

Make like the preceding, using 1 tablespoon of chopped chives or shallots, or green onion tops instead of chopped onion.

### GREEN BEAN SALAD

Put a can of good "stringless" beans on the ice an hour before wanted, open, drain, and arrange in a salad bowl with 2 teaspoons of grated or finely chopped onion and 1 cup of French dressing. Serve ice-cold.

### BEET SALAD WITH CELERY

Cut boiled beets in thin slices and use a vegetable cutter to cut them into fancy shapes. Mix 1 cup of beets with 1 cup of thinly sliced celery, cover well with mayonnaise, serve on lettuce leaves.

### CABBAGE SALAD

Slice firm white cabbage as thin as possible, then cut it across, mix it with mayonnaise dressing, and serve on small white cabbage leaves.

### CELERY AND PINEAPPLE SALAD

Use equal parts of thin strips of celery and shredded pineapple. Select a perfectly ripe pineapple. Put the celery and pineapple each by itself, and place on the ice. When time to serve mix them together with mayonnaise, garnish with celery leaves, and serve at once.

## CHERRY SALAD

When fresh cherries are available they are best, but the large cherries in glass bottles are also suitable. Remove the stones from fresh cherries, and in their places put blanched filberts or hazelnuts. Put on curled lettuce leaves with a tablespoon of green mayonnaise on each.

## CUCUMBER SALAD

Soak 2 unpeeled cucumbers in ice-cold water for twenty minutes or more, then peel and use a patent scraper on the sides to serrate the edges, or do this by drawing a silver fork firmly down the length of the cucumber; this will make the slices have fancy edges. Slice, and arrange with small white lettuce leaves in a salad bowl. Cover with French dressing and add a sprinkling of paprika to the salad itself before serving. Some sliced radishes may be added if liked.

## COUNTRY SALAD

Use 1 cup each of finely sliced firm white cabbage, diced celery, and chopped apple; mix them well with mayonnaise dressing, and serve in the inner leaves from the cabbage.

## RUSSIAN CUCUMBER SALAD

Prepare like plain cucumber salad, but put with the sliced cucumbers 1 small onion sliced thin, with the slices separated into rings. One tablespoon of chives may be added, or more chives used and the onion slices omitted.

## DENT DE LION SALAD

Take young dandelion leaves, trim off all the stem below the leaf, and mix with a French dressing to which has been added onion juice or chopped chives; use 1 tablespoon of either to each cup of dressing. Hard-boiled eggs, sliced or chopped, are sometimes used to garnish this salad.

## PINK EGG SALAD

Boil 6 or 8 eggs for ten minutes, put in cold water for two or three minutes, then peel and put in a jar of pickled beets, well covered with vinegar. Let them stand a few hours and serve with the beets.

## ENDIVE SALAD

Wash heads of endive and use the crisp, white, light leaves. Shake dry and cover with French dressing. Add 1 teaspoon of minced onion before dressing.

## FETTICUS OR CORN SALAD

Wash 2 cups of fetticus and dry the leaves well, then cover with French dressing, and add 1 teaspoon of grated onion.

## GARDEN SALAD

Take a handful of sorrel, 2 sprigs of chervil, 4 leaves of tarragon (or use tarragon vinegar), 1 teaspoon of chopped chives, and the small leaves from the heart of a head lettuce. Blend all well with French dressing.

## GRAPE-FRUIT SALAD

Wash and shake dry the fine leaves from a head lettuce, and arrange with them in layers very thin slices of grape-fruit; mix well with French dressing before serving.

## ITALIAN SALAD

Having prepared 2 nice heads of head lettuce, arrange them in the salad bowl with 2 seedless oranges which have been neatly peeled, and cut into thin slices with a very sharp knife. Season with salt and pepper, and then mix thoroughly with French dressing. The oranges and lettuce should have been chilled so that the salad will be very cold.

## LETTUCE SALAD

Pull apart a fresh head lettuce, breaking the leaves neatly from the stalk, and wash those that need it and shake them dry. Put in a salad bowl with French dressing or sauce vinaigrette, and mix well together before serving.

## MACEDOINE SALAD

Open a glass or can of imported macedoine of vegetables, drain, and cover with French dressing. Arrange with lettuce leaves in a bowl or on separate plates. Freshness can be added by a tablespoon of chopped chives, or shallots, or parsley.

## SPECIAL MIXED SALAD

Use 1 cup of chopped tomato, 1 cup of chopped cucumber, ½ cup of thinly sliced radishes, ½ cup of chopped apple, and 2 tablespoons of the German pearl pickled onions. Mix all together with 1 cup of mayonnaise, and arrange in a salad bowl with lettuce leaves, which should be used to hold the salad in serving.

## MUSHROOM SALAD

Select fresh, firm mushrooms that are small, wash them carefully without peeling, and stir them in French dressing that contains rather more oil than usual. Put 1 crisp lettuce leaf on each plate, fill it with the mushrooms, sprinkle with salt and a little paprika, and serve very cold.

## NARRAGANSETT SALAD

Wash and shake dry the fine white centre of endive or chicory, and arrange with it quartered tomatoes from which the skin has been removed; serve with a French dressing to which a tablespoon of chopped parsley, ½ teaspoon of chopped onion, and 1 finely chopped egg has been added.

## PHILADELPHIA SALAD

Select large tomatoes, remove the skins by putting in boiling water, cut out the inside, and refill with finely chopped pineapple, celery, and apple in equal proportions, all well blended with plain mayonnaise. Serve on lettuce leaves on separate plates, or use watercress instead of lettuce.

## PIMENTO SALAD WITH CHEESE BALLS

Mix 2 Neufchâtel cheeses with 1 cup of grated cheese, and when creamed together add 6 olives stoned and chopped fine and 1 teaspoon of chopped pimento; season generously with salt and pepper, moisten with cream, and mould into balls an inch and a quarter through. Pimolas (which are olives stuffed with pimentos) can of course be used if more convenient, and a few drops of onion extract or a very little onion juice adds piquancy to the cheese balls. Take lettuce which has been in cold water and is therefore crisp, shake it dry, and arrange with it pimentos cut in long half-inch strips, mix thoroughly with a French dressing, and garnish with the cheese balls.

## POLISH SALAD

Use boiled beets, sliced and mixed with French dressing, and over all sprinkle chopped white of hard-boiled egg.

A little grated horse-radish is sometimes used with good effect in beet salad.

## GERMAN POTATO SALAD

Boil 6 medium-sized potatoes, and after draining shake them over the fire a moment or two to dry; then peel and slice while warm, and cover at once with a dressing made of 1 teaspoon of salt, 1 saltspoon of black pepper, 1 tablespoon of chopped parsley, 1 chopped onion, 5 tablespoons of oil, and 3 tablespoons of vinegar. Mix and let stand on ice for an hour or so, then put with crisp lettuce leaves in a salad bowl, and garnish with chopped boiled or pickled beets.

## RED POTATO SALAD

Use equal quantities of boiled beets (canned ones are convenient) and boiled potatoes. Dice both and mix well together, adding 1 tablespoon of vinegar. Let stand until the potatoes are reddened, then add 1 tablespoon of grated onion, mix well with French dressing, and garnish with slices of hard-boiled egg. Place in a salad bowl, with fine white cabbage or crisp lettuce leaves.

## ROMAINE SALAD

Pick over crisp heads of romaine, let stand a few minutes in cold water, then shake until dry, and serve with French dressing to which grated onion is added, using 1 teaspoon of it to each cup of dressing.

## SOUTHERN SALAD

To 2 cups of cold boiled rice add 2 chopped hard-boiled eggs and blend well with mayonnaise. Arrange on crisp lettuce leaves with a garnish of egg slices, and beet, and sliced olives.

## SORREL SALAD

A refreshing salad may be made from the sorrel found growing wild. Wash it well, cut the stalks off, and dredge with salt, pepper, celery salt, and then mix with oil, and sprinkle well with tarragon vinegar and a little grated onion.

## AMERICAN POTATO SALAD

Mix cold sliced boiled potatoes with mayonnaise dressing and add 1 tablespoon of capers.

## SPANISH SALAD

Remove the skins from large, solid tomatoes and 1 small cucumber, take the seeds from 1 small sweet green pepper, pare 1 small Spanish onion, and cut all in slices, making the peppers extremely thin. Mix with 1 tablespoon of chopped nasturtium leaves or stems or seeds, and cover with French dressing, mixing well. Let stand on ice an hour before serving. Serve with cheese balls.

## SUNDAY-NIGHT SALAD

Wash 1 large head of crisp head lettuce, separate the leaves, rejecting all but perfect ones, and shake them dry. Put them in a large salad bowl, and with them put 1 onion chopped very fine, 5 sliced tomatoes, and the leaves from 3 or 4 sprigs of watercress. At the table dredge the salad generously with salt, and sprinkle with black pepper, covering the entire surface; then pour from an oil bottle 3 or 4 tablespoons of oil over the vegetables slowly, and follow this with about 2 tablespoons of vinegar; add 1 tablespoon of tarragon vinegar, then dredge with celery salt, and add a little cayenne, and mix all together with a wooden fork and spoon, turning the whole mass over and over ten or more times. The bowl may be well rubbed with garlic and the onion omitted.

## RUSSIAN TOMATO SALAD

Slice 5 or 6 very small tomatoes, and put with them 2 onions sliced and divided into rings. Cover with French dressing.

## SLICED TOMATO WITH CHIVES

Slice 4 tomatoes, put with them 3 tablespoons of chopped chives, and cover with French dressing. Serve on lettuce leaves.

## WALDORF SALAD

Use 1 cup of shelled walnuts, broken or chopped, 1 cup of diced tart apple, 1 cup of crisp celery cut in small pieces, and mix well with mayonnaise dressing. Serve on curly lettuce leaves.

## WATERCRESS SALAD WITH ORANGES

Cut two inches off the bottom of a bunch of watercress with a sharp knife, wash the cress thoroughly in ice-cold water, drain, and arrange in a salad bowl with 3 seedless oranges cut in thin slices, and mix all together with a dressing made of 1 tablespoon each of tarragon vinegar, olive oil, and brandy; season well with salt and pepper, and serve very cold.

Grape fruit can be substituted for the orange, or equal amounts of orange and grape fruit used.

## YOKOHAMA SALAD

Cut into small cubes 2 fresh cucumbers that have been on ice until chilled and then peeled, and put with them 1 diced sour apple, 1 tablespoon of shredded pimentos, 1 small bunch of watercress (using the leaves only), and 2 tablespoons of chopped mint leaves. Mix with French dressing and serve on lettuce leaves.

A SALAD SUPPER

Use large dinner plates, and on each arrange 6 of the large light green leaves from the inner part of head lettuce, putting 5 of them with the stalk-end toward the centre of the plate, and another small one in the centre. Fill the centre leaf with radishes (cut like roses) and olives, and fill the others as follows: In one put 2 tablespoons of canned green beans, well mixed, before putting on the leaf, with a little grated onion and French dressing, on the second put 3 or 4 slices of tomato and 2 teaspoons of mayonnaise, on the third arrange 3 stalks of canned asparagus (white preferred) dipped in French dressing and sprinkled with chopped chives, on the fourth put 2 half-lengths of a quartered cucumber to be dipped in salt in eating, and on the fifth put 1 tablespoon of tiny German pearl onions, 2 pickled walnuts, and 2 gherkins. Serve nut or plain bread, or creamed cheese sandwiches, or all three. This supper may be varied in many ways; one is to use potato salad or beet and egg instead of the beans. This as it stands was the result of an emergency when six persons were suddenly to be served to a late supper and no preparation made. A well-stocked store-room of preserved goods and a small kitchen garden filled the need.

# SAVOURIES

The savoury begins a meal well, and is a convenient dainty for late suppers. The variety is practically endless, and those given here may be altered and added to indefinitely.

FRESH MUSHROOM "COCKTAILS"

Put a small handleless cup or glass in the centre of a plate and encircle it with 6 of the smallest white leaves of lettuce. On each leaf place 2 small white firm button mushrooms, which have been freshly gathered and carefully washed but not peeled. Fill the cocktail glass three quarters full of sauce made of ½ cup of tomato chutney, 1 teaspoon of lemon juice, 2 drops of tabasco (more if liked very hot), and ½ teaspoon of salt. Set the plates in the refrigerator for half an hour. Deliciously prepared "Cocktail" sauce can be purchased in bottles.

## CANNED MUSHROOM "COCKTAILS"

In each cocktail glass put 8 or 10 button mushrooms, and cover them well with the cocktail sauce. Or use canned cêpes and serve in green pepper cases.

## PIMENTO "COCKTAILS"

Cut squares, an inch across, from sweet pimentos (canned), and put 8 or 10 of these in each glass; cover well with cocktail sauce and serve ice-cold, with celery.

## BEET SAVOURY

Use 1 large pickled beet and arrange neat slices on squares of bread; in the centre of the beet put a ring of hard-boiled sliced egg, filled with the riced egg-yolk, and fill each corner with chopped chives.

## BEET AND EGG SAVOURY

Chop equal parts of pickled beet and the whites of hard-boiled eggs together, and arrange on toast or bread with the riced yolks of the eggs, mixed with a little chopped chives or parsley, in a cone on the centre. Season well.

## BROWN-BREAD SAVOURY

Cut brown bread into shapes, spread with butter, then heavily with cream cheese containing some salt, and cross two evenly cut strips of pimento on each piece of bread thus prepared. At the juncture of the strips of pimento place a slice of pimola, and put one in each space on the cheese. Sprinkle with paprika, and put a few capers here and there.

## CUCUMBER SAVOURY

Cut bread in rounds and arrange on it neat slices of cucumber, the edges serrated before slicing by drawing a silver fork lengthwise of the cucumber. Sprinkle with salt and paprika, and on each slice put a ring from a small sliced onion, or arrange instead the tiny German pearl pickled onions between the slices of cucumber. Sprinkle a little lemon juice over to serve. A variation is made by using chopped chives only, or each ring of onion may be filled with them.

## CREOLE SAVOURY

Toast one side of shaped pieces of bread, and butter the untoasted side, and on it spread a layer of chopped tomato mixed with half as much chopped green pepper and some salt. Put in the oven or under the gas flame for five minutes, and upon removing arrange a cone of finely chopped onion in the centre of each.

## EGG SAVOURY

Use fresh bread slightly toasted or less soft bread without toasting. Cut in squares, diamonds, or rounds, and sprinkle with Worcestershire sauce, or any good sauce, then cover neatly with the chopped whites of hard-boiled, well-salted eggs, on which arrange a centre of the riced yolks. Put a round slice from a black pickled walnut on each corner, dot with capers, and sprinkle with paprika.

## HORSE-RADISH SAVOURY

Spread oblong pieces of bread thinly with mustard, cover with a layer of chopped whites of hard-boiled eggs mixed with a little grated horse-radish, arrange capers in strips crosswise of the bread, and between these sprinkle the hard-boiled yolks of the eggs which have been riced or pressed through a sieve. At the corners and in the centre place thin slices of gherkins.

## MUSTARD SAVOURY

Cut shaped pieces of bread and spread with made mustard. Cover them with chopped hard-boiled eggs mixed with a little chopped chives. Arrange capers in lines or any pattern on this. Season well.

## NEUFCHÂTEL SAVOURY

Mix Neufchâtel cheese with ¼ as much butter and rub to a cream, and then squeeze through a tube onto salted, hot crackers, forming star-like rosettes. Sprinkle with paprika, garnish with capers.

## ONION SAVOURY

Use shaped pieces of bread and spread thinly with butter, then arrange a quarter-inch layer of finely minced Spanish onion mixed with chopped parsley and slightly dampened with tomato sauce; put in the centre of each the ring of a slice of hard-boiled egg, with a slice of pickled walnut fitted into it.

## PICKLE SAVOURY

Spread any savoury sauce and then cream cheese on oblong pieces of bread, and arrange on this thin slices of small sour pickles in a neat row, lengthwise. Sprinkle with paprika.

## STUFFED OLIVE SAVOURY

Arrange on squares of bread spread with tomato or any tart sauce strips of riced yolk of hard-boiled egg; form squares by placing them both ways of the bread, and in each put a ring of the white of hard-boiled egg sliced, and fill the centre with a slice of pimola or any other stuffed olive.

## CAPER SAVOURY

Make same as the above using capers to fill the egg rings.

## TOMATO MAYONNAISE SAVOURY

Chop tomatoes and mix with them a thick mayonnaise, either plain or flavoured with herbs. Spread on shaped pieces of bread, and garnish with thin rings sliced from green peppers.

## TOMATO SAVOURY

Cut rounds of bread the size of the tomatoes to be used and toast one side; then butter the other side and arrange on each a slice of tomato, dredge with salt, pepper, and dry mustard, sprinkle with mushroom catsup or walnut catsup, and set under the burners of a gas stove for five minutes or until heated but not softened. Garnish with watercress to serve.

## LIPTAUER SAVOURY

Spread shaped pieces of bread with "Liptauer cheese" and garnish with slices of pickle.

## SWEET PIMENTO SAVOURY

Toast fresh bread slightly, cut into shapes and butter one side, and on this arrange a trimmed piece of canned Spanish pimento sprinkled with celery salt, and set under the gas flame of a gas stove for five minutes to heat.

## ROUNDS OF TOAST

To make rounds of bread or toast take an empty tin the size required and press it firmly into a slice of bread, thus cutting the round evenly and neatly.

Cutters for cutting vegetables into fancy shapes are convenient for savouries.

# SANDWICHES

The recipes given under Savouries can also be used in making sandwiches, and originality can have full play here as in the making of dainty and appetising savouries.

### SAVOURY BUTTER SANDWICHES

Use unsalted or slightly salted butter, and with a silver knife press into it any flavour desired,—onion juice, paprika, various sauces, chopped peppers, or capers,—using 1 teaspoon of minced herbs, etc., to each tablespoon of butter. Spread in sandwiches.

### PROVIDENCE HOUSE CLUB SANDWICHES

Cut fresh bread in medium thick slices, trim the four edges, and butter it with butter somewhat softened by warmth. On one side of two slices which belong next to each other put thinly sliced peeled tomatoes, filling in bits to cover the bread neatly. Press 4 or 5 slices cut from pickled walnuts into the juicy parts of the tomatoes, lay 6 or 7 capers also in, and use half a teaspoon of the tiny German pearl onion pickles to each sandwich. Sprinkle with salt, pepper, and celery salt, and spread with mayonnaise. Press the other piece of bread firmly on, and wrap in waxed paper for picnics.

Vary with chopped chives, tarragon leaves, French dressing, etc.

### APPLE SANDWICHES

Arrange thinly sliced, cored apples between layers of buttered bread from which the crust has been cut. Sprinkle with salt and spread with mayonnaise, into which a few chopped nuts have been mixed.

## CREOLE SANDWICHES

Trim and butter squares of bread and fit to them thinly sliced tomatoes, and spread with thin mustard; slice green peppers very thin, and arrange sections of the rings here and there over the tomatoes. Use a little minced chives or shallot, or onions, and season with salt and pepper and lemon juice or some sauce.

## BOMBAY SANDWICHES

Spread squares of bread with curry paste, and cover with chopped tomato to which is added a little chopped onion and the same amount of chopped sour apples. Season with salt.

## PEANUT-BUTTER SANDWICHES

Spread small oblong pieces of bread, from which the crust is cut, with peanut butter blended with cream, and press firmly together.

## EGG SANDWICHES

Break 2 eggs into a frying pan containing a little melted butter and let them spread, breaking the yolk with a spoon after they are in the pan; let them fry until the edges begin to brown, then season with salt and pepper, and sprinkle with chopped chives. Cut pieces out to fit the bread slices to be used, and, after trimming and buttering the bread, arrange them on one side of the sandwich. Use with no other flavouring, or sprinkle with Worcestershire sauce, or spread with mustard. Wrap in waxed paper for picnics.

## NUT SANDWICHES

Mix chopped nuts in thick cream or mayonnaise, and spread between slices of bread, either with or without a lettuce leaf. Sprinkle with cayenne.

## LETTUCE SANDWICHES

Spread oblong slices of trimmed bread with butter, lay a lettuce leaf between, trimmed to size, and spread with plain or green mayonnaise.

## PIMOLA SANDWICHES

Butter small squares of bread and arrange on them sliced pimolas or any stuffed olives, sprinkle with lemon juice, or spread with mayonnaise.

## PICKLE SANDWICHES

Slice large pickles and arrange them between buttered bread slices. If German Dill pickles are used and German flavours liked sprinkle with caraway seeds, and use rye bread.

## CHEESE SANDWICHES

Cut American or Swiss cheese very thin, spread with mustard, and place a piece, trimmed to the size of the bread used, between two pieces of buttered white or rye bread.

## GERMAN SANDWICHES

Use rye or "black" bread, with caraway seeds baked in it, spread the two slices with unsalted butter, and on one arrange thin slices of Swiss cheese; spread this with German or French mustard, and arrange on it 2 or 3 slices of Dill pickles.

## HONOLULU SANDWICHES

Pare and core 3 apples, stem and seed 2 sweet green peppers, and put them through a vegetable mill. Mix them into 2 Neufchâtel cheeses, and use as filling for brown or white bread sandwiches.

# PASTRY, PATTY CASES, Etc.

## PIE-CRUST

Shortened pie-crust is made by using for one pie ⅔ of a cup of flour, with ⅓ of a teaspoon of baking powder and ¼ of a teaspoon of salt in it. Sift this onto ½ a cup of cocoanut butter or ½ a cup of butter, or these two in equal proportions, dampen with ice-water, and roll out five or six times. Keep ice-cold until used.

## EASY PUFF PASTE

Use a chopping bowl for mixing the paste, and into it put 4 cups of flour (sifted), 1 tablespoon of sugar and 1 teaspoon of salt, adding it a spoonful at a time. Use 2 cups of butter, chopping it into the flour until it is as fine as possible. Beat 2 eggs for five minutes and add to them the juice of one lemon and ½ cup of very cold water, and stir this gradually into the paste. When mixed lift the paste to a well-floured pastry board, roll it into a rectangular shape, fold it over onto itself from the four sides, then roll again, and repeat this process four times. Now fold into a thin piece of linen, and place on a plate near the ice in the refrigerator, and let it stand half an hour or more. Roll out again and use for patties, or pie-crust.

## TIMBALE CASES

Make a batter of ¾ of a cup of flour, ½ cup of milk in which 1 egg has been beaten, 1 teaspoon of sugar, 1 saltspoon of salt, and at the very last add 1 tablespoon of olive oil. Dip the timbale iron in the batter, then in hot vegetable fat, taking care it does not touch the bottom of the pan. When a golden brown remove and place on paper to drain, and proceed thus until a sufficient number has been made. Fill with chestnuts, mushrooms, etc., in sauce, and reheat in the oven after filling.

## BATTER FOR FRITTERS

Make as for timbale cases and dip the vegetables or fruit to be fried in it, and fry until golden brown in hot fat.

## PASTRY FOR PATTY PANS OR CASES

Instead of frying-batter for timbale cases a paste can be made with 1½ cups of flour, 1 egg-yolk, and 3 tablespoons of butter well-mixed and dampened to the proper consistency by using perhaps ½ cup of cold water. Roll out very thin, about 1/16 of an inch, and press into the small pans or moulds after buttering them. Trim neatly, and press a little cup of buttered tissue paper in each, fill this with rice to protect the inside from too much heat and to keep flat on the bottom, and bake in a rather slow oven. Do not turn out until cooled, and do not fill until wanted.

Ordinary pastry may be used also to line moulds for patty cases, timbales, etc.

## POTATO CRUST

Boil good-sized potatoes with the skins on, peel while hot, and press through a ricer or sieve, mix with an equal quantity of white flour or whole wheat flour and a little salt, and dampen with cream. Press together and roll out for top crust of vegetable pies.

## ESSEX PASTRY

Mix equal parts of mashed potato and flour pastry, and use baked in small squares as a garnish, or as a covering for deep vegetable pie.

## DUMPLINGS

Sift 2 cups of flour, add to it 1 heaping teaspoon of baking powder and ½ teaspoon of salt, and sift again. Stir into this 1 scant cup of milk, or just enough to make a dough that can scarcely be handled without sticking to the fingers. Drop in boiling vegetable stock or into a stew and let boil rapidly ten minutes, taking great care not to uncover the kettle until just as the dumplings are removed. Serve at once in the stew or with brown sauce.

## CROUTONS

Cut slices ¼ of an inch thick of stale bread, and with a knife cut across both ways to make tiny squares. Dry a few moments, then toss in a little hot butter to brown and serve warm.

## BREAD CRUMBS

A jar of bread crumbs should always be kept on hand. Use stale bread, break it into bits, and brown it slightly in the oven. Then with a roller, or in a mortar, crumble it and crush it to powdered crumbs. If a jar of light crumbs and one of golden brown crumbs are kept ready, they will be found most convenient.

# A FEW HOT BREADS

## BAKING POWDER BISCUITS

Take 2 tablespoons of butter and sift onto them lightly 2 cups of flour in which 1 heaping teaspoon of baking powder is mixed, and with freshly washed, cool hands mix the flour and butter thoroughly together, then pour on slowly, stirring with a wooden spoon, 1 cup of milk; with most flours this cup of milk or a very little less will make the biscuit dough of the proper consistency, but if too thin or too thick, judgment must be used, as the dough should be so that with well-floured hands it can scarcely be handled, but can with rapid motions be made into a roll which will keep its shape when put on a well-floured bread board. It should then be rolled lightly with a roller to the thickness of three quarters of an inch, and with a biscuit cutter, the edge of which should be dipped in flour before using, cut the rounds quickly out and place them at once in a shallow buttered pan and set in the oven. They should be properly cooked in eighteen or twenty minutes. The smallest sized baking powder tin is exactly the right size for a biscuit cutter.

This same recipe makes dumplings, strawberry short-cake, and the top of vegetable pies.

## POP OVERS

Mix 1 saltspoon of salt with 1 cup of flour, and add slowly enough from 1 cup of milk to just make a smooth paste; stir this well, then add the remaining milk and the beaten yolk of 1 egg, and then the white whisked to a stiff froth. Put the batter in buttered gem pans or earthenware cups, and cook in the oven about twenty-five minutes, or until browned and standing very high. Serve at once.

## GRAHAM GEMS

Mix 2 cups of whole wheat flour, ½ teaspoon of salt, 1 tablespoon of sugar, and stir onto this 1 cup of milk containing the beaten yolks of 2 eggs, then add the beaten whites of the eggs, and put in hot buttered gem pans. Bake about twenty-five minutes.

## TENNESSEE CORN BREAD

Beat 2 eggs in a mixing bowl, add 1 heaping teaspoon of granulated sugar, and 1 cup of milk; mix ½ cup of white flour, 1 cup of yellow corn meal, and 3 teaspoons of baking powder, and sift these into the milk, stirring constantly. The batter should be thin enough to spread readily when poured into the inch-deep baking pan. Just before pouring in the batter put 1 tablespoon of butter in the baking tin and when it melts, stir the batter into it; this is the secret of crisp brown bottom crust and was learned from an old negro cook. Bake twenty minutes to half an hour or until tinged with brown.

## SOUTHERN RICE MUFFINS

With 1 cup of boiled rice put 1 cup of milk, 1 tablespoon of butter, the beaten yolks of 2 eggs, 1½ cups of flour, 1 tablespoon of sugar, ½ teaspoon of salt, and 1 heaping teaspoon of baking powder. After mixing well add the well-beaten whites of the eggs, pour into hot buttered gem pans, and bake in a quick oven from twenty to twenty-five minutes.

## RICE GRIDDLECAKES

Mix well together 2 eggs, 2 cups of milk, ½ teaspoon of salt, 1 tablespoon of sugar, 2 cups of flour, 2 teaspoons of baking powder, and 1½ cups of boiled rice. Bake on a hot buttered griddle, browning both sides.

## CORN CAKES

In 1½ cups of sour milk put 1 teaspoon of soda, 1 beaten egg, 1 tablespoon of sugar, 1 teaspoon of salt, 1 scant ½ cup of white flour, and thicken with enough yellow corn meal to make a thin batter. Fry a golden brown on a hot buttered griddle.

## WHEAT CAKES

Beat 2 eggs lightly and pour over them 2 cups of milk; mix 2 teaspoons of baking powder with 2 cups of flour and ½ teaspoon of salt, and sift lightly into the milk, stirring constantly. Cook in small pancakes on a hot buttered griddle.

## GINGERBREAD

Beat the yolks of 2 eggs lightly, melt ½ cup of butter and add to the eggs, then stir in ½ cup of milk, 1 teaspoon of soda, and 1½ cups of dark molasses. Then add slowly 3 cups of sifted flour and 1 tablespoon of ginger, and after beating the whites of the eggs to a stiff froth stir them in with a fork. Bake in an inch-deep baking pan in a slow oven for three quarters of an hour.

## SUNDAY MORNING WAFFLES

Beat 2 eggs thoroughly, and add to them 2 cups of milk and 1 saltspoon of salt, and sift into the milk 2 cups of flour containing 2 heaping teaspoons of baking powder, stirring constantly. Some flour thickens more than others, and if more must be added sift it before stirring in. The secret of the excellence of waffles is not getting the batter too thick; it must spread readily when put upon the iron but not run. Melt 1 tablespoon of butter and put it in the batter at the last moment. Butter the hot waffle iron, using a bristle brush an inch or so wide for the purpose, over half-fill the iron with batter (using a large spoon), let one side brown, and then turn, to brown the other. Divide into the four parts indicated by the iron and serve with maple syrup.

# PLUM PUDDING AND MINCE PIE

## PLUM PUDDING

Blanch 1 cup of almonds and ½ cup of Brazil nuts, and put them through a fine grinder; add to them 1 cup of blanched chopped walnuts, and mix with these 2 cups of very fine bread crumbs, ½ cup of butter, ½ cup of brown sugar, the grated rind of 3 lemons (washed well before grating), 2 cups of seedless raisins, 2 cups of currants, 2 cups of light Sultana raisins, 1 cup of mixed candied peel finely shredded, and when well blended stir into this six slightly beaten eggs and 1 teaspoon of salt. Put in a pudding basin and steam or boil for eight hours; boil several hours to reheat the day it is to be used. Serve with brandy sauce and nun's butter.

## PLUM PUDDING SAUCE

Beat 1 egg until very light, stir into it 1 cup of sugar, and when blended add 3 tablespoons of boiling water and cook over boiling water for five minutes, adding 1 wineglass of brandy during the last two minutes' cooking.

## NUN'S BUTTER

Beat ½ cup of butter until creamy, and add slowly to it 1 cup of powdered (or granulated) sugar. Add 1 tablespoon of vanilla, lemon, or brandy, and a sprinkling of grated nutmeg.

## MINCE PIE

Bake 3 large apples, and press them through a sieve to remove skins and cores; grate the rinds from 3 lemons, and add this and the juice of the lemons to the apple pulp; wash, pick over, and bruise in a mortar 1 cup of currants; stone 2 cups of raisins, and cut them in slices. Mix these all well together, chop into them 1 cup of butter (or cocoanut butter), a little salt, 4 cups of brown sugar, 1 tablespoon of candied lemon peel, 1 tablespoon of candied citron, and 1 tablespoon of candied orange peel, all well minced, and after stirring well, add 2 tablespoons of orange marmalade and ½ cup of good brandy. Put in sealed glass jars, cover with wax or brandied paper before the jar is closed, and use for pies in two weeks.

www.ingramcontent.com/pod-product-compliance
Lightning Source LLC
Chambersburg PA
CBHW081624100526
44590CB00021B/3587